The Talent Review Meeting Facilitator's Guide

Cover Art by Jeremy Sims

Editorial Review by Julie Rael

To order additional copies or customized versions of this book, contact Succession Builders, LLC at 214-906-3155 or doris@successionbuilders.com.

www.SuccessionBuilders.com

AuthorHouse™
1663 Liberty Drive
Bloomington, IN 47403
www.authorhouse.com
Phone: 1-800-839-8640

© 2010 Doris Sims, SPHR. All rights reserved.

No part of this book may be reproduced, stored in a retrieval system, or transmitted by any means without the written permission of the author.

First published by AuthorHouse 7/27/2010

ISBN: 978-1-4490-2880-0 (sc)

Library of Congress Control Number: 2009909482

Printed in the United States of America

This book is printed on acid-free paper.

Because of the dynamic nature of the Internet, any Web addresses or links contained in this book may have changed since publication and may no longer be valid. The views expressed in this work are solely those of the author and do not necessarily reflect the views of the publisher, and the publisher hereby disclaims any responsibility for them.

authorHOUSE®

Dedicated with love

To my brothers and sisters

Dale and Leslie

Dean and Jennifer

TABLE OF CONTENTS

Section One: What Is Talent Management? 9
    Talent Management—Typical Job Responsibilities 10
    Talent Management Concepts 11
    Talent Concepts: Similarities and Differences 12
    Talent Management Terms 12
    The Business Need for Talent Management 15
    Make Informed Talent Decisions and Reduce Risk 16
    Talent Management: A Win-Win for Everyone 17
    Keep Your Sales and Leadership Pipelines Full! 18
    The Leadership Pipeline 19
    Past Performance and Future Potential 20
    Identify Talent Resources to Achieve Business Goals 21
    Talent Management Forces 22

Section Two: The Talent Review Meeting 25
    Talent Review Meeting Best Practices 26
    More Talent Review Meeting Best Practices 27
    Three Phases of the Talent Review Meeting Process 28
    Attributes of Talent Review Meeting Facilitators 29
    Your Role as the Talent Management Project Lead 30
    Establishing Internal Talent Management Policies 31
    The Roles of Your Talent Review Meeting Partners 32
    Working with Human Resource Partners 33
    Working with the Meeting Scribe 34
    Working with Business Leaders and Assistants 35

Section Three: Planning the Talent Review Meeting 37
    Defining Your Goals 38
    Defining Your Talent Review Meeting Scope 39
    Defining Your Talent Management Timeline 40
    A Sample Annual Talent Review Timeline 41
    A Sample Multi-Year Talent Management Plan 42

TABLE OF CONTENTS

Identify Your Talent Meeting Discussion Topics 43
Sample Talent Meeting Agenda.. 45
Sample Meeting Ground Rules 46
Definitions: What is a High Potential? 47
Definitions: What is a Successor? 48
Definitions: What is a Key Expert?.. 49
Begin to Design a Development Program Now... 50
Planning the Length and Logistics of the Meeting 51
Calculating the Length of the Meeting... 52
Case Example: Planning a Talent Review Meeting.. 53
Case Example Worksheet 54
A Facilitator Preparation Checklist.. 55

Section Four: Talent Assessment and Preparation 57

Talent Assessment Tools 58
A Tool for Managers: Employee Career Discussions 59
Consistency is Key 60
Defining Talent Assessment Tools 61
Talent Assessment Tools: The Talent Profile 62
The 9-Box Chart 63
Position Competency Models 64
Career Growth Descriptions 65
Identifying Critical Positions 66
Talent Assessment: Rating Leadership Competencies 67
Case Example: Analyzing Leadership Assessment Data 68
What System Will You Use?.. 69
Talent Management Communication Ideas... 70
Business Leader Content for Communications 71
Sample: A Quick Reference Tool for Business Leaders... 72
Talking Points for Leaders 73
Preparing the Senior Leader for the Meeting 75
Talent Review Meeting Logistics 76

TABLE OF CONTENTS

Section Five: Facilitating the Talent Review Meeting 77
- The Roles of the Talent Meeting Facilitator.. 78
- Facilitation Tips: Keeping the Meeting on Track 79
- Questioning Techniques for Facilitators 80
- Sample Talent Review Discussion 81
- Documenting the Meeting – Scribe Responsibilities 85
- Scribe Notes Example 86

Section Six: After the Talent Review Meeting 87
- Sample Questions – Post Talent Review Evaluation 88
- Talent Review Meeting Facilitator Feedback Form 89
- High Potential Notification: You Have Choices! 90
- A Sample Talent Notification Process 91
- What Do They Need to Know? 92
- How Do I Develop High Potential Employees? 93
- Leadership Development Ideas—Be Creative! 94
- Case Example: Making Development Recommendations.. 95
- Case Example: Development Recommendation Notes... 96
- Talent Management Metrics 97
- Communicate Your Results 98

Appendix 99
- Talent Management Concepts: Same and Different 100
- Case Example: Planning a Talent Review Meeting... 101
- Case Example: Analyzing leadership assessment data 102
- Case Example: Development Recommendation Notes... 103
- Frequently Asked Questions... 104

HOW TO USE THIS GUIDE

The purpose of this book is to provide practical advice, ideas, and tools for individuals who are responsible for leading Talent Review Meetings within their own organization. This book is designed to save you time by providing basic checklists and templates for documents to be used before, during and after your Talent Review Meetings.

Use this book as your planning guide to help you, your team and your Business Leaders to be fully prepared for the Talent Review Meeting process. Use the information in the book to think through your strategy and processes. Use the checklists to track your action plan progress. Use the templates as a foundation to create your own Talent Review Meeting communications and documents.

To request volume orders of this book, customized versions of this Guide, and additional training and consulting go to www.SuccessionBuilders.com for contact information.

This book does not provide legal advice. Readers are advised to work with professional legal counsel to review and approve all talent assessment, succession planning, and leadership development strategic plans, processes and programs created, modified, and/or implemented within their own organizations.

ABOUT THE AUTHOR

About the Author: Doris M. Sims, SPHR is the Founder and President of *Succession Builders, LLC*, a talent management, succession planning, and new talent onboarding consulting firm. Her experience in organizational development spans over 20 years.

Doris has implemented leadership development, talent management strategies, and new employee orientation programs in Fortune 100 and Fortune 500 companies in healthcare, finance, telecommunications, and information systems, including Alcatel, First Horizon Home Loans, and Caremark. She received her Master's degree in Human Resource Development from Indiana State University.

Doris is the author of **The 30-Minute Guide to Talent and Succession Management** and the coauthor of **Building Tomorrow's Talent: A Practitioner's Guide to Talent Management and Succession Planning**. She is also the author of the McGraw-Hill book **Creative New Employee Orientation Programs**, and has contributed articles to many other McGraw-Hill books and multiple periodicals, including *Training Magazine, Talent Management Magazine,* and *The Consultant's Toolkit*.

Doris has served as a speaker at multiple national and international conferences since 1999, including *International ASTD conferences, Training Director's Forum, Training Magazine conferences, HR Southwest,* and *International Quality and Productivity* conferences.

As Talent Management Director of Caremark, Doris' talent management strategy and processes were featured as best practices in the 2005 **Learning & Development Roundtable** publication: **Profiles of Leadership Development Tactics**. In 1996, Doris received the *Outstanding Performers in Training Management* award, in the category of "Establishing a New Training Function", from *Training Director's Forum Newsletter* and Lakewood Publications.

Since 2004, Doris has also served on the Board of Directors for the non-profit organization *Communities in Schools of North Texas* (www.cisnt.org). For more information go to **www.SuccessionBuilders.com**, or e-mail Doris Sims at **doris@successionbuilders.com**.

SECTION ONE
WHAT IS TALENT MANAGEMENT?

The definition and scope of the term Talent Management may vary within organizations of different sizes, with different cultures and different business needs. One company may be focusing on succession planning to ensure a strong pipeline of leaders to fill pending retirement vacancy positions, while another organization might be focusing on the identification of high potential employees to develop future leaders and key employees to lead a growing start-up company. However, we can all use a basic definition of Talent Management as:

A focus on the onboarding, identification, assessment, development, and movement of internal talent.

The **objectives** of a Talent Management strategy may include:

- Identification of emerging talent to fill high vacancy risk roles and future leadership needs
- Development of specific competencies to ensure emerging talent is prepared for future roles in the organization
- Retain key talent and critical expertise within the organization
- Identify talent risk areas and develop contingency plans and succession plans
- Increase diversity within the key talent and leadership populations of the organization
- Decrease the high costs associated with external recruiting
- Develop more cross-functional career movement and job experiences within the organization, to avoid a "silo-mentality" that focuses only on upward advancement within one functional area
- Provide a structured and consistent focus on talent development and purposeful career movement in the organization
- Talking with employees about their talents and development interests, and increasing their own accountability and ownership of their career growth

What additional objectives would you include for your organization?

TALENT MANAGEMENT—TYPICAL JOB RESPONSIBILITIES

Some organizations use the term talent management to refer to both external talent recruiting and to internal talent identification. Both external talent acquisition and internal talent management are designed to identify top talent for the organization. However, the focus of **internal** talent management pertains more to the retention and development of talent, rather than sourcing new talent externally. In addition, the skill sets of employees in **external** talent recruiting roles (talent acquisition) are very different from those who are responsible for internal talent management, as shown below:

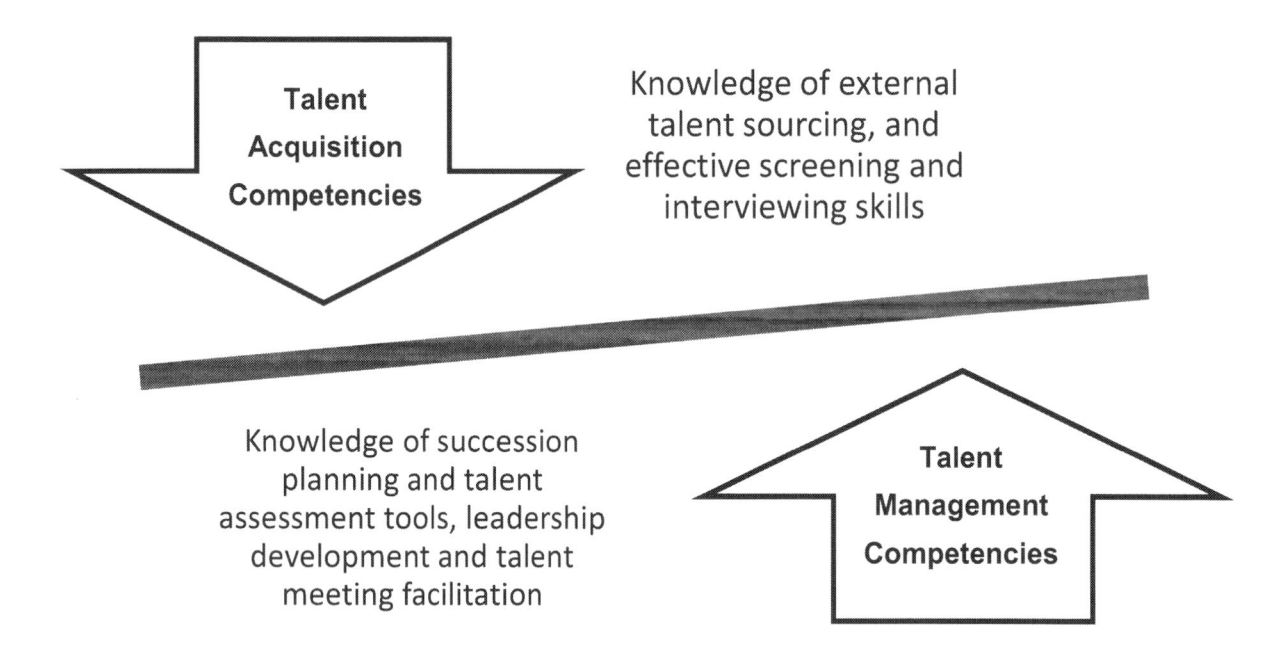

Talent Acquisition Competencies: Knowledge of external talent sourcing, and effective screening and interviewing skills

Talent Management Competencies: Knowledge of succession planning and talent assessment tools, leadership development and talent meeting facilitation

In small organizations, the Talent Management Professional's job responsibilities may include both internal and external talent responsibilities. However, in mid to large sized organizations, there is a strong case to be made for the creation of a Talent Management role to focus solely on internal talent management, which may include some or all of these job functions:

- **Succession Planning**
- **High Potential Employee Identification and Development**
- **Leadership Development**
- **New Employee Orientation and Onboarding**
- **Career Movement and Job Rotational Assignments**
- **Performance Management**
- **Talent Assessment Processes**
- **Talent and Organizational Review Meetings**
- **Key Expert Employee Identification and Retention**
- **Workforce Planning and Organizational Design**

TALENT MANAGEMENT CONCEPTS

To fully understand talent management, it is important to clarify the similarities and differences between this concept and other human resource strategies that are often associated with talent management.

Understanding these differences can help you to explain these terms to your Business Leaders, and to answer questions and concerns you may receive from the employees you serve.

How would you define the **similarities** and **differences** between each of the terms in the table below?

Talent Management	⇔	Performance Management
Successors	⇔	High Potentials
High Potentials	⇔	High Performers

TALENT CONCEPTS: SIMILARITIES AND DIFFERENCES

To fully understand Talent Management, it is important to clarify the similarities and differences between these concepts and other organizational strategies that are often associated with talent management. **Use the worksheet below to document your ideas about the differences between each concept. Find suggested answers in the Appendix of this book.**

Talent Management ⇔ **Performance Management**

<u>How are they similar</u>? Both are designed to review and enhance employee performance.
Document their differences below...

Successors ⇔ **High Potentials**

<u>How are they similar</u>? Both are designed to improve the company's leadership pipeline.
Document their differences below...

High Performers ⇔ **High Potentials**

<u>How are they similar</u>? Both are critical to the success of the organization.
Document their differences below...

See sample responses to this exercise in the Appendix of this book.

TALENT MANAGEMENT TERMS

360-Assessment – An on-line survey and/or personal interview process designed to obtain feedback from those who work and interact with an employee on a regular basis. Feedback is obtained from the employee's manager, peers, and direct reports.

Blocker – A position within the organization in which the employee occupying the role lacks advancement ability or desire, and is also in the direct development path of a promotable employee.

Development Plan – A process and tool for determining and recording the specific development actions in support of an employee's leadership development.

Fatal Flaw – Refers to behaviors that might cause a person to be unsuccessful in a leadership role. Examples include lack of interpersonal skills, lack of integrity, etc.

High Performer – An employee who consistently demonstrates superior work performance, but does not currently demonstrate a strong ability or desire for rapid advancement, career challenges and risks, and/or leadership roles.

High Potential – A High Performer employee who also consistently demonstrates high potential for career movement into multiple growth positions, and the ability and desire for rapid advancement into leadership roles.

Leadership Benchstrength – Refers to the competency and readiness levels of leaders to grow with the organization and to be prepared for new leadership roles. Organizations with a strong leadership benchstrength have multiple successors actively developing in the pipeline (both short and long term successors) to fill current and future leadership roles, as well as high potential employees with the desire and ability to move into multiple potential current positions and into positions that may be created in the future.

Leadership Competencies – The knowledge, skills, and abilities attributed to effective leaders, defined by the organization to reflect the leadership values, culture, and business needs of the company. Best in class organizations identify specific sets of leadership competencies that are unique to the organization's culture, business needs, and values. These competencies can be used in performance management and talent management initiatives to identify and develop leaders within the framework of the organization's competencies.

Learning Agility – Learning agility encompasses the ability to learn very quickly and think creatively. Leaders with high learning agility also seek out the ideas and feedback of others, and work towards continuous improvement both for personal effectiveness and team effectiveness. Demonstrating high learning agility includes the ability to be flexible, handle stress well, adapt to change, and to work effectively in ambiguous situations.

TALENT MANAGEMENT TERMS (CONTINUED)

Talent Assessment – A manager's evaluation and appraisal of an employee based on past performance and future potential.

Talent Management – Facilitating the development and career progress of highly talented and skilled employees in the organization, using formalized processes and tools.

Talent Profile – A source of employee information which often includes educational background, work history, major accomplishments, career aspirations, willingness to relocate, and other personal information useful in guiding the leadership team in job placement and development decisions.

Talent Review Meeting – A meeting facilitated by either a Human Resources Professional or a Business Leader to review the strengths, development areas, and potential career paths of employees and leaders in the organization, as well as discussing position vacancy risks and successors for current and future roles in the organization.

Workforce Planning – Working with Business Leaders to identify the number of employees required to meet business requirements, the types of positions to be added or eliminated to meet business goals, and the recruiting or reduction-in-force efforts that will be required in specific time periods to ensure compliance with budget and customer needs.

THE BUSINESS NEED FOR TALENT MANAGEMENT

The business practice of talent and succession management is still relatively new and is expanding and growing as an important Human Resource function. In today's world, the talent in your organization is a key differentiator between your organization and your competitors.

Your talent creates your products and services, serves your customers, and manages the important strategy and administration of your organization every day.

This is why top companies know:

> **Just as we continuously review our finances and future budget resource needs . . .**
>
> . . .So should we also continuously review our emerging leaders and future talent resource needs.

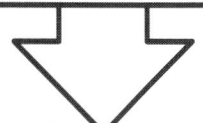

⬇

> **Just as we identify and develop new products, services and new market growth . . .**
>
> . . . So should we identify and develop high potential employees and successors for leadership growth.

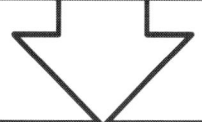

⬇

> **Just as we continuously communicate with our investors, partners and stockholders . . .**
>
> . . .So should we also continuously communicate with employees about their career interests, relocation ability, and their next job assignments.

Every day Business Leaders use processes and tools to help make the best decisions possible – running a business successfully is both an art and a science. No "perfect" business tools and decision-making processes exist, but these tools help leaders make more informed decisions. In addition, business tools and processes are designed to reduce risk.

MAKE INFORMED TALENT DECISIONS AND REDUCE RISK

Every day Business Leaders use processes and tools to help make the best decisions possible – running a business successfully is both an art and a science. No "perfect" business tools and decision-making processes exist, but these tools help leaders make more informed decisions. In addition, business tools and processes are designed to reduce risk.

Examples of these processes and tools used by leaders on a regular basis to 1) analyze data, 2) and 3) make informed decisions include:

Mergers and Acquisitions: The Due Diligence Process

New Product Development: Market Analysis

Advertising: Focus Group Feedback

Hiring New Employees: The Interview Process

Developing New Technology: User Requirements Analysis

Developing and Promoting New Leaders: Talent Assessment and Succession Plans

---

Talent assessment and succession planning processes are business tools that are also designed to 1) analyze talent data, 2) make informed talent development decisions, and 3) reduce risk (leadership vacancy risk).

While you will not see 100% of your successor candidates filling open positions as they become available, you can expect your internal fill of open positions to increase, your retention of top talent to increase, and your position vacancy risks and external recruiting costs to decrease.

As you lead the talent management strategy, you are spending valuable time discussing the strengths, development needs, potential career movement and action plans for the most valuable assets of your organization—your people.

TALENT MANAGEMENT: A WIN-WIN FOR EVERYONE

Talent assessment and succession planning processes are business tools that are also designed to analyze data, make informed decisions, and reduce risk (leadership vacancy risk). While you will not see 100% of your successor candidates filling open positions as they become available, you can expect your internal fill of open positions to increase, your retention of top talent to increase, and your position vacancy risks and external recruiting costs to decrease.

Talent Management is good for the company and good for employees, as shown below:

Advantages to Employees	Advantages to the Business
The process enables you to communicate and "brag on" your top talents, past work experience, and competencies	Just as you assess other business risks and form contingency plans, the process assesses and plans for talent vacancy risk
You can be assured that your leaders are discussing you career interests with you and working with you to plan a potential career path	The process provides a forum, a timeslot and a structure to discuss talent and performance as a leadership team
Your development actions will be designed to leverage your strengths and develop areas that the entire leadership team recommends for you	Think of the process as a "talent inventory" that raises the visibility of top talent, identifies positions with missing successors, and plans for the future talent needs of the organization

So how will Talent Management save you money?

- **You will decrease your external recruiting costs and fees**
- **Your retention of top talent and performance will increase**
- **You will decrease the costs of onboarding and training new employees**
- **Your "time-to-fill" for open positions will decrease**
- **Your key position vacancy risk decreases**

IMPORTANT: Be sure to obtain baseline metrics before you implement or enhance your talent management strategy so you can accurately measure your future results.

KEEP YOUR SALES AND LEADERSHIP PIPELINES FULL!

What does it really mean to have a strong leadership pipeline?

First, think of a successful sales group. The organization will have new customer markets they are just looking into, potential customers they are contacting for the first time, prospective customers who are in the sales process, customers they are about to close the deal with, and current customers.

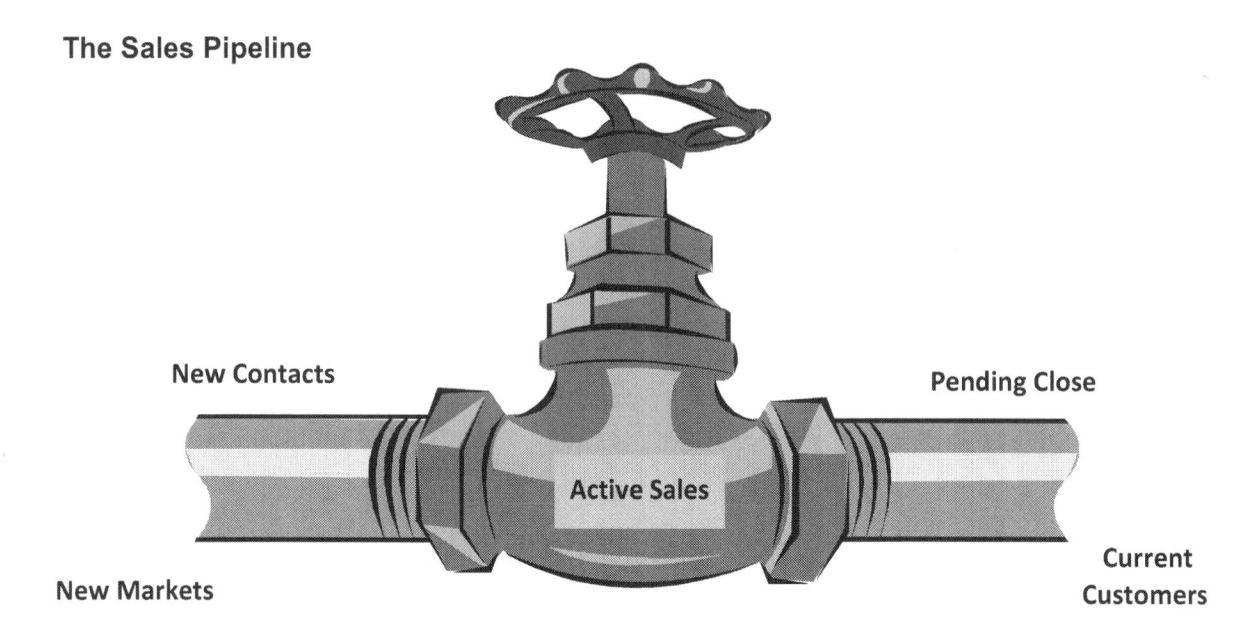

The Sales Pipeline

New Contacts

Pending Close

Active Sales

New Markets

Current Customers

Consider what would occur if there were any gaps in the <u>sales pipeline</u>:

- If new markets and new contacts are not pursued, current markets become saturated
- If active and pending sales slow, the organization knows that future financial results will be impacted
- If the organization loses current customers, there is an immediate financial impact to the company and to shareholder perceptions

If any part of the pipeline is weak, it will affect the company's financial position sooner or later. This is why every successful Business Leader reviews every aspect of their sales pipeline continuously to keep it full at each point in the sales process.

THE LEADERSHIP PIPELINE

The concepts of the Sales Pipeline can be applied to your <u>Leadership Pipeline</u>:

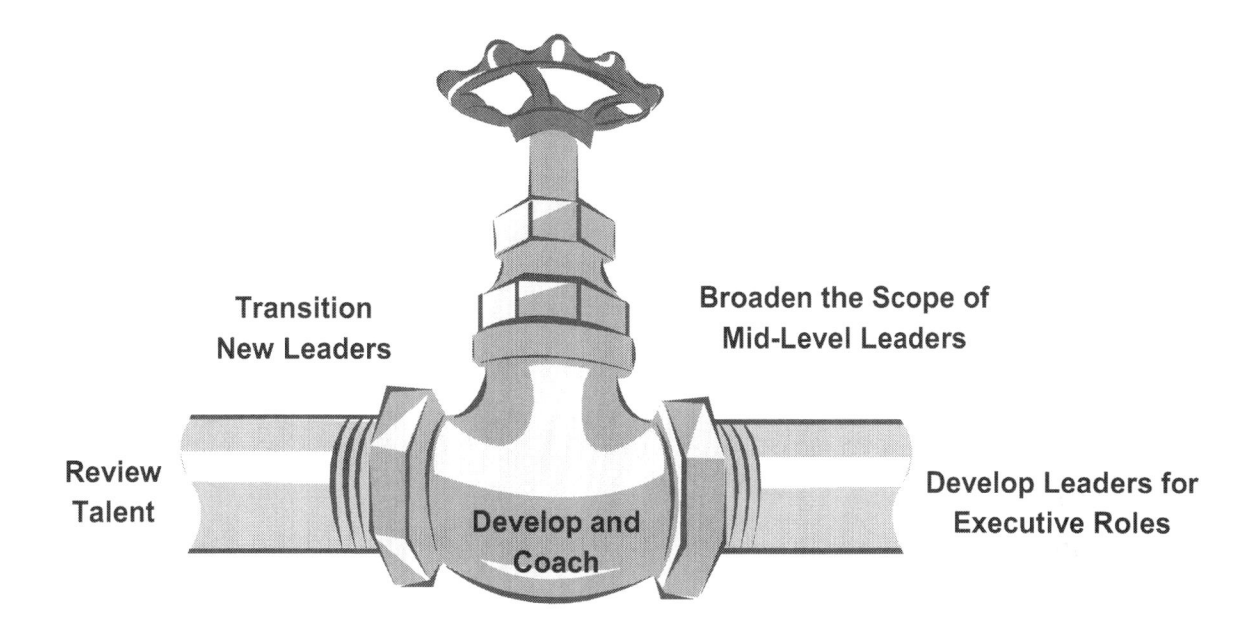

```
        Transition              Broaden the Scope of
        New Leaders             Mid-Level Leaders

Review                                              Develop Leaders for
Talent          Develop and                         Executive Roles
                Coach
```

- Just as you continue to review new markets for your products and services, it is important to review and develop your "internal new talent markets" – your current individual contributors who could be your next front-line supervisors and managers

- Develop your current leaders to broaden their scope, strategic thinking, and people skills

- Continue to develop your senior leaders to develop a pool of prepared future executives

- Just as losing a key customer would have an immediate impact in the company, the loss of a key executive also has an immediate impact in the organization both externally and internally, so it is critical to retain key talent and to identify and develop successors

An effective sales department continuously reviews each phase of their sales cycle to ensure there are no "clogs" or gaps in the pipe. The sales department knows that if the gap is not addressed, it will impact business results sooner or later. The same concept applies to the leadership pipeline—if we don't review and develop top talent and leaders continuously, the clog in the pipe will eventually surface as a vacant leadership position without a prepared successor ready to take on a new challenge.

PAST PERFORMANCE AND FUTURE POTENTIAL

Most organizations already do a great job of reviewing their PAST performance and their FUTURE potential when it comes to their **financial resources**. Imagine an organization that stops creating and reviewing financial reports and ends their budgeting processes!

When considering your talent management strategy, are leaders held to the same level of accountability for their **talent resources** as they are for the financial resource requirements and processes of the organization?

The chart below compares financial and talent processes—how we look at our past performance and how we predict future resource needs. Most companies have well-established processes, systems, and accountability associated with the three dark gray boxes, but the actions associated with Predicting Future Potential of Talent Resources is still an emerging function in many organizations.

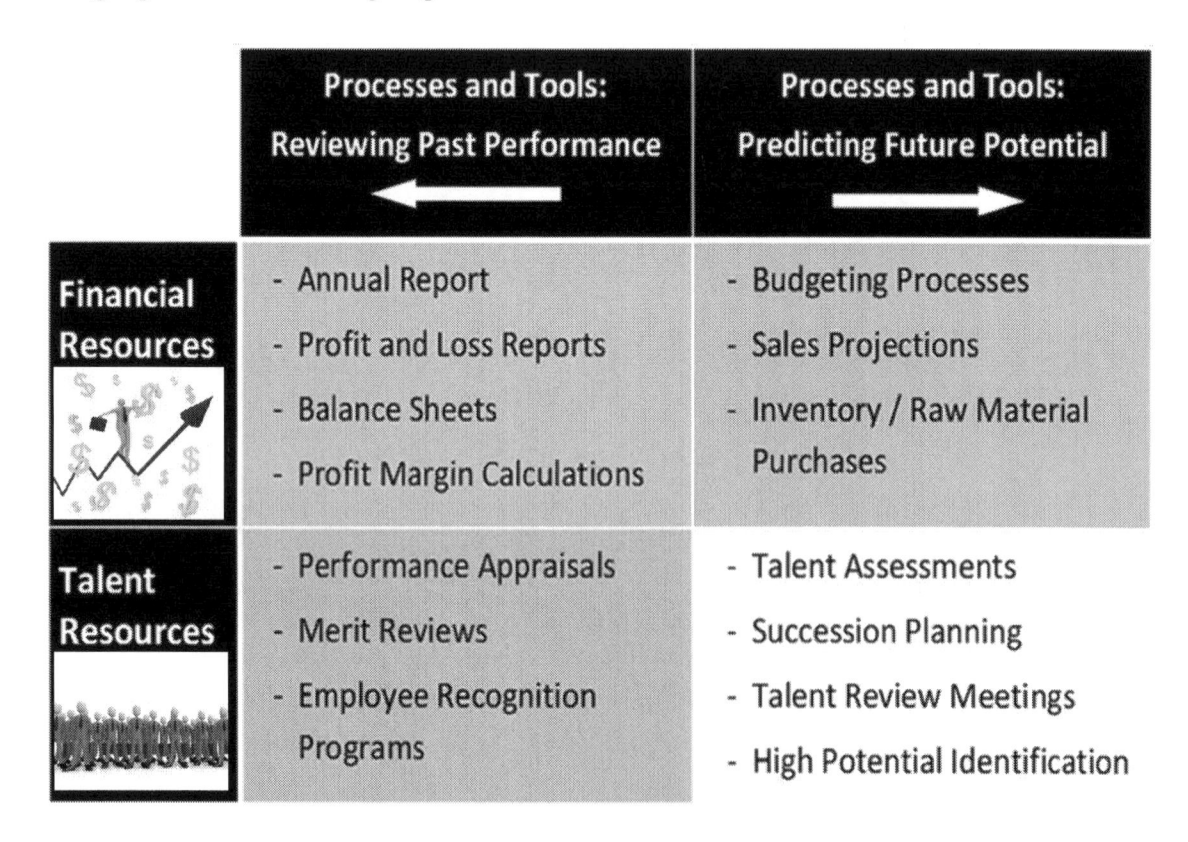

	Processes and Tools: Reviewing Past Performance ←	Processes and Tools: Predicting Future Potential →
Financial Resources	- Annual Report - Profit and Loss Reports - Balance Sheets - Profit Margin Calculations	- Budgeting Processes - Sales Projections - Inventory / Raw Material Purchases
Talent Resources	- Performance Appraisals - Merit Reviews - Employee Recognition Programs	- Talent Assessments - Succession Planning - Talent Review Meetings - High Potential Identification

As we review the left side of the chart—**Reviewing Past Performance**—we see that most organizations have many processes and tools in place to measure both the financial results and the talent results in the company. As we look at the right side of the chart—**Reviewing Future Potential**—we see that virtually all organizations spend a large volume of time (and have tools, processes and accountability in place) pertaining to budgeting and other financial projections, but many organizations spend limited time and resources predicting future talent needs.

The vision for effective talent management is to bring the same level of time, tools, processes and accountability in place to review our talent resources as we do our financial resources.

IDENTIFY TALENT RESOURCES TO ACHIEVE BUSINESS GOALS

When leaders develop their budgets each year, they identify and request the **FINANCIAL RESOURCES** they will need to achieve those goals.

Similarly, the Talent Management process enables leaders to identify the **TALENT RESOURCES AND ACTIONS** needed to achieve their goals. An example of this thought process is shown below:

Business Goal
Increase customer satisfaction ratings

People Resources
- Hire (or promote from within) a new Customer Service Vice President to lead this goal
- Increase number of customer service representatives by 5%

Retention, Motivation and Movement
- Determine cause(s) of high turnover among Customer Service Managers
- Modify Performance Appraisal form to include customer satisfaction goal
- Move the current Call Center Director into an other role

Training and Change Management
- Review and revise our training program for new customer service representatives
- The new Customer Service Vice President will present the new goal and strategy at each location

As the leader of your Talent Management strategy in your organization, work to ensure the strategy is designed to meet the corporate business goals. This will shape the scope of your strategy; for example, if your key goal is to identify potential successors to develop for leadership vacancy position risks due to pending retirement issues, the scope of your Talent Management project may focus on these specific roles, and/or you might only focus on a group of specific leadership roles in the company, such as all Vice President positions and above.

However, if your key goal is to identify new management trainees to prepare for future first-line management positions in the company, the scope of your project will actually focus on high potential individual contributors in the organization.

TALENT MANAGEMENT FORCES

Every corporate initiative or project will have forces that help drive the project to successful results, and every project will also have risks or restraints that can threaten the success of the strategy. Your Talent Management strategy is an example of this type of initiative.

Use the chart below to identify the forces in your organization that will work to help you successfully implement your Talent Management strategy, as well as the potential obstacles that might stall or reduce the effectiveness of your strategy.

Once these potential Drivers and Restraining Forces are identified, work with your Talent Management project team to determine action plans that will leverage the project's strengths and mitigate risks.

Talent Management Drivers →	← Talent Management Restrainers

Talent Management Effectiveness Action Plans

After completing the Force Field analysis exercise on the previous page, use the worksheet below to document the actions your project team can take to strengthen your driving forces and to reduce the risks and potential obstacles associated with your restraining forces.

What we will do: **Who will lead this action:**

What we will do: **Who will lead this action:**

What we will do: **Who will lead this action:**

What we will do: **Who will lead this action:**

What we will do: **Who will lead this action:**

SECTION TWO
THE TALENT REVIEW MEETING

In this chapter, we'll discuss the Talent Review Meeting purpose, as well as the three phases of the Talent Review Meeting process. We will also review the roles and responsibilities of each team player in the process, and how to work most effectively with each of your internal project partners throughout the project timeline.

What is a Talent Review Meeting?

A Talent Review Meeting is a face-to-face meeting of Business Leaders to review the strengths, development areas, and potential career paths of the talent (employees and leaders) in the organization, as well as discussing position vacancy risks and successors for current and future roles in the organization.

The Talent Review Meeting is also designed to...

- Increase the *VISIBILITY* of talent in the organization
- Increase the *VALIDITY* of the Succession Plans, High Potential Identification and Development Action Plans

The Talent Review Meeting increases the visibility of talent in the organization, as the leaders are sitting down to focus on reviewing the competencies, work experience, education, career interests, leadership ability, etc. of the people who are already in the organization.

Without the Talent Review Meeting process, many times an organization may not be aware of a talented employee who could fill an open or future position, and therefore the company spends the time and money to source and hire an external individual for these roles. Employees see this, and become frustrated that their management team is not aware of their strengths and competencies, and retention of key talent becomes a challenge.

Conversely, when leaders spend time discussing career interests and abilities with employees and employees are aware of the talent management strategy, retention increases as employees see that their job growth is an important business process in the organization. Visibility of available internal talent increases, internal fill of open positions increases, and employee engagement and retention increases.

The Talent Review Meeting increases the validity of the decisions regarding high potential identification and succession plans, because the process is designed to obtain data regarding the observations and perspectives of multiple leaders in the company, rather than basing talent management decisions on a single manager's perspective or a single rating system.

TALENT REVIEW MEETING BEST PRACTICES

The Talent Review Meeting is most effective as a face-to-face meeting. A Talent Review Meeting is most effective as a face-to-face meeting with Business Leaders to discuss the talent needs to achieve business goals and the talent resources and development required to achieve those goals.

Typically a Talent Review Meeting is too long and too important to be held as a virtual session, such as a phone or video conference meeting. However, if a Talent Review Meeting attendee must participate virtually, ensure the individual is in a secure location, as the content and discussions of the meeting are often highly confidential.

The Talent Review Meeting should be led by an objective and trained facilitator. Ideally, the facilitator of the meeting should stay in an objective role throughout the meeting. Remaining in an objective role increases the trust of the participants that the facilitator is a "true translator" of their discussion and decisions. Even if the facilitator is an internal employee, he or she must demonstrate the ability, the confidence, and the objective perspective to be able to ask challenging questions and to help the Business Leaders think through the talent discussions and development action plans.

Just as you would provide training for an individual prior to facilitating a workshop for the first time or providing 360-feedback coaching for the first time, another best practice is to provide training (formal or on-the-job training) to individuals before they lead their first Talent Review Meeting. The Talent Review Meeting is one of the most visible phases of the Talent Management process, and it requires an individual with the confidence and ability to lead a meeting with participants who are often in much "higher-level" positions in the organization.

Who Should Facilitate Talent Review Meetings?

One question to consider is whether the meeting should be facilitated by a Human Resources Professional or by a Business Leader. There is no clear best practice pertaining to this question, but we can compare the advantages of each approach:

Advantages of a Human Resources Facilitator	Advantages of a Business Leader Facilitator
• An HR facilitator is much more likely to lead the meeting as an objective facilitator	• Increases the "ownership", understanding and accountability of Business Leaders of their own talent management strategy and processes
• An HR facilitator serves to ensure the meeting follows consistent and legally defensive human resource procedures	• Increases the number of individuals available to lead Talent Review Meetings in the organization
• An HR facilitator is able to facilitate meetings throughout the organization, gathering cross-functional talent data throughout the company	
• An HR facilitator serves to ensure the meeting decisions are well documented and that action plans are identified and recorded	

MORE TALENT REVIEW MEETING BEST PRACTICES

The most effective talent meeting facilitators demonstrate the following competencies:

- Credibility and a trust level with the leaders and executives (due to the nature of the discussions that will take place during the meeting)

- Confidence and ability to appropriately challenge and question talent identification and development discussions

- The ability and professional presence to lead a meeting

- The ability to "read between the lines" of discussion, and to ask questions that will increase the clarity, validity, and richness of talent data

- Overall knowledge of the business goals, talent needs of the organization, and of the talent management strategy and process of the organization

The Talent Review Meeting should provide a formal "timeslot" and structure for talent discussions. During a Talent Review Meeting, it becomes clear that managers have a lot of information about the talent in their organization that is often not being used or addressed with action plans. Just as Business Leaders frequently meet to discuss budget issues and financial projections, so should the organization set aside time specifically to discuss the talent resources in the company.

The Talent Review Meeting should balance a tone of candor and cooperation. A Talent Review Meeting is ineffective if leaders don't speak openly and honestly about talent needs, high potentials, successors and performance issues during the meeting. There are times when a Talent Review serves to provide the time to discuss either an exciting high potential individual who is critical to the organization, or an individual with a performance issue that is currently not being addressed—everyone is aware of the issue but no one is taking action to correct the situation. So the candor of a Talent Review discussion is very important to achieve the business purpose of the meeting.

Conversely, a Talent Review Meeting should never become a "free-for-all" discussion with aggressive discussions, conflict and adversity. The facilitator of the meeting and the meeting participants should continuously work to ensure the discussion focuses on win-win results for the organization and on the big picture—what is best for the entire organization? There are two key ways to help achieve this balance of candor and cooperation:

- Review Talent Meeting Ground Rules at the beginning of the meeting (locate sample Ground rules on page 46 of this book)

- Distribute a written Talent Review Meeting Agenda at the beginning of the meeting and ensure the discussions of each individual reviewed in the meeting are fair and consistent (locate a sample Agenda on page 45 of this book)

The Talent Review Meeting should provide a forum for <u>multiple perspectives</u> regarding the potential of individuals and ideas for career path options. For this reason, it is important to have multiple Business Leaders in a Talent Review Meeting who have data points and a perspective on individuals discussed in the meeting, and to have the Human Resource business partner participate in the meeting discussions as well.

THREE PHASES OF THE TALENT REVIEW MEETING PROCESS

The Talent Review Meeting is part of a process that can be defined in three distinct phases:

1. **The Preparation Phase—Talent Assessment:** The Talent Review Meeting is preceded by the Talent Profile entry or update process (including a meeting with the employee), and a Talent Assessment process, in which managers review the past performance and future potential of each employee to be discussed in the Talent Review Meeting.

2. **The Calibration Phase—Talent Review Meeting:** The Talent Review Meeting is the "calibration step" in which leaders come together to discuss vacancy risk, leadership strengths, development plans, succession plans, etc. and agree upon strategic talent decisions and succession plans.

3. **The Follow-Up Phase—Development Plans and Accountability:** The Talent Review Meeting is followed by the finalization of succession plans and high potential populations, the creation of Development Plans, and the follow-through of development actions throughout the year.

Preparation: Profile Updates, Career Discussions, Assessments	Calibration: Talent Review Meetings	Follow Up Actions: Analysis/Recommendations Development Plans

Consider what would occur if any one of these three phases is eliminated:

Without the Preparation Phase, leaders come to the Talent Review Meeting unprepared to answer questions about the career interests, leadership abilities and relocation desires of employees. The facilitator has no data to review prior to the Talent Review Meeting, and the meeting is significantly less effective as it is starting with a blank slate.

Without the Calibration Phase, the process of identifying potential leaders for advancement reverts back to our previous practice in which individual managers determine promotions without considering objective data and the opinions of other leaders in the business unit. The visibility of talent is significantly reduced in the organization.

Without the Follow-Up Phase, Talent Review Meeting action plans are not communicated or executed to employees, and the crucial development to prepare leaders as successors and as future leaders of the organization is forgotten. Without follow-up and accountability, the entire process is seen as something that "sits on a shelf" without achieving business results. Each phase is critical to the success of your Talent Management strategy!

ATTRIBUTES OF TALENT REVIEW MEETING FACILITATORS

Definition: The Talent Review Meeting Facilitator is responsible for ensuring all data, meeting documents, and other logistics are prepared for the meeting. The facilitator reviews the meeting agenda, process, and ground rules.

The facilitator is the leader of the meeting, responsible for ensuring the meeting stays on track, and uses skilled questioning techniques. The most effective talent meeting facilitators demonstrate the following competencies:

- **The most important trait** of an effective Talent Review Meeting Facilitator is to be perceived as credible and trustworthy in the view of the leaders and executives who attend the meetings (due to the nature of the discussions that will take place during the meeting)

- The facilitator must also demonstrate confidence and the ability to appropriately challenge and question talent identification and development discussions

- The facilitator must be fully prepared for the meeting and must demonstrate a professional presence to lead the meeting

- Talent Review Meeting Facilitators must learn to develop the ability to "read between the lines" of discussion, and to ask questions that will increase the clarity, validity, and richness of talent data

- The facilitator should demonstrate knowledge of the business goals, talent needs of the organization, and of the talent management strategy and process of the organization

YOUR ROLE AS THE TALENT MANAGEMENT PROJECT LEAD

You are the leader of the Talent Management strategy in your organization. Your role is critical to the success of the organization's talent processes, and your Business Leaders look to you for direction and support as they execute their talent management actions.

To serve most effectively as the leader and facilitator of the Talent Management strategy in your organization, you will need to:

- **Identify the business goals** and strategic objectives of the Talent Management strategy

- **Identify sponsors or champions** of the strategy who will help with funding, communications and support

- **Identify your internal team members** who will play a role in executing the plans

- **Define and execute the project implementation plan** to execute the strategy

- **Provide training and information** as needed to Business Leaders and internal partners to ensure everyone is prepared for the Talent Review Meeting process

- **Facilitate Talent Review Meetings** with your Business Leaders

- Assist managers with the creation and execution of their employees' **development plans**

- **Analyze talent data**, prepare reports, recommendations and/or presentations to communicate talent strengths and risks

- Identify and communicate organizational and leadership development **recommendations** based on the Talent Review Meeting results

- Work with Business Leaders and other Human Resource Professionals to **obtain development resources for action plan follow up**

- **Work with the Recruiting team** to facilitate career movement and to use talent and succession management data to provide qualified internal applicants

ESTABLISHING INTERNAL TALENT MANAGEMENT POLICIES

Part of your preparation process is to ensure that internal talent management policies and processes are in place to be followed after you identify successors and high potential employees. Most companies have some internal job posting processes in place already (such as the length of time a job will be posted internally) but the identification of high potentials and successors creates new questions and issues to be resolved.

Just as you have consistent policies and procedures that your Human Resource partners and your Business Leaders follow for every external candidate who applies for and interviews for a position in your company to ensure compliance with employment law, the same is true for your internal recruiting (talent management) processes when you fill positions internally. The absence of consistent policies and procedures for internal career movement and promotions can cause morale problems and even potential litigation.

Some internal talent management questions to consider to form internal talent management policy include the following (consult with your legal department or outside counsel for advice regarding your decisions):

1. Will high potentials and successors be given any priority over other candidates for open positions in the company?

2. Since we have already identified prepared successors for some positions, should we still post these jobs internally to provide an opportunity for others to apply?

3. If a manager is interested in a high potential employee for his or her team, can the manager contact the employee directly, or should the manager first contact either the high potential employee's manager, and/or the Human Resources or Talent Management department?

4. If a good internal job assignment opportunity arises for a high potential employee but his or her current manager says the employee is required to achieve an important business goals and doesn't want the employee to be moved, who will make this decision?

5. If the company requires job assignments (domestic or global) as part of their high potential development program, how long should the employee stay in the job assignment before being eligible to move to another position?

6. Are there any circumstances in which we will communicate to an employee that he or she is a successor to be developed for a position in which there is a known vacancy in the future to enhance the development process?

7. Typically, one of the goals of a talent management process is to increase internal fill of positions and decrease the "time-to-fill" of open positions. However, sometimes a manager has a desire to "hold on" to an employee and lengthen the transition time period to the new job. Should a limit be placed on this transition time period?

8. Will we establish reward structures for managers who excel at promoting the development and internal career movement of their employees?

THE ROLES OF YOUR TALENT REVIEW MEETING PARTNERS

As the leader of your organization's Talent Management strategy, you are the central figure in the planning and implementation of the strategy. But you will need help from others who will assist you in communicating, funding, and executing the talent strategy.

The Talent Management Project Lead and the supporting partners of this process will vary based on the size, structure and needs of your organization. For example, in a smaller organization, the Talent Management Project Lead might also be the Organizational Development lead, the Recruiting Lead, and the HR Partner, requiring the individual to wear multiple hats. In larger organizations, an effective design of the Talent Management team includes the following roles:

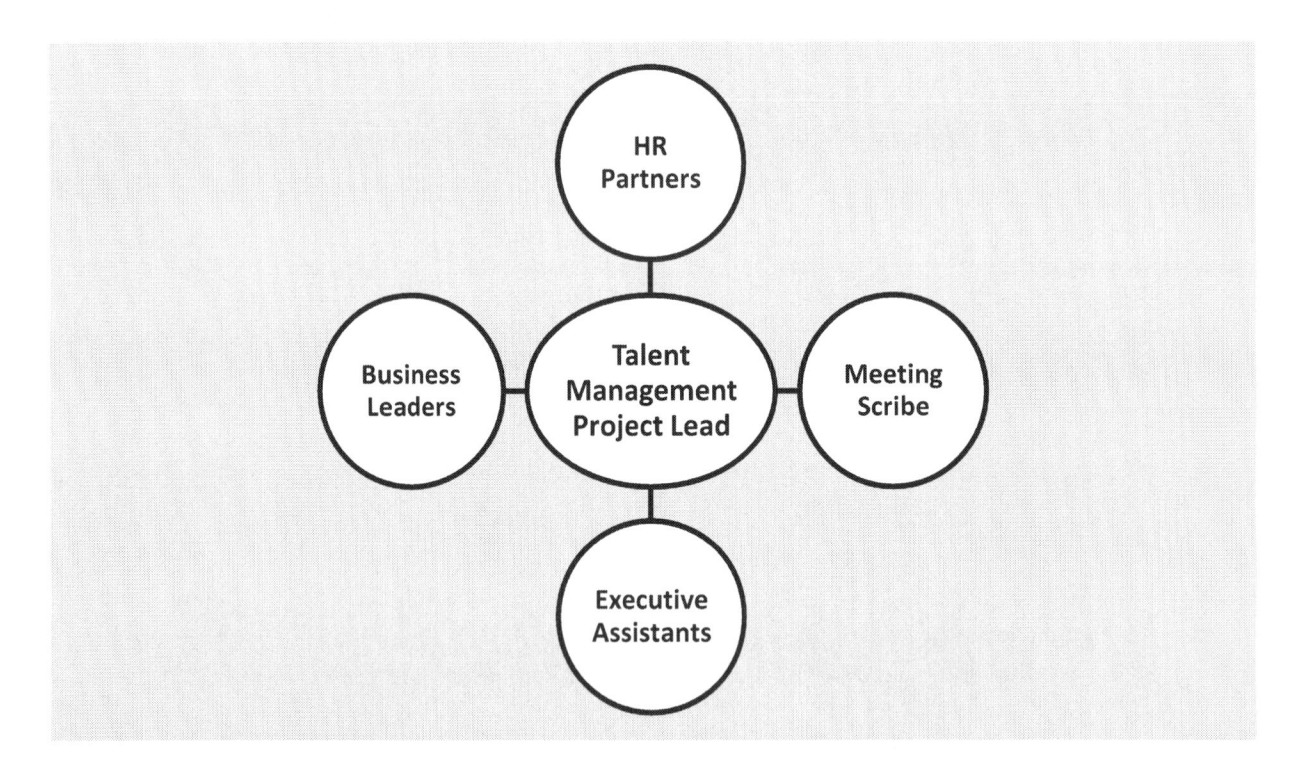

In this section, we'll discuss the roles, action plans and best methods of working with each of your internal partners in the Talent Review Meeting process:

Human Resource (HR) Partners—This may include HR Business Leaders associated with specific business functions, and it may include colleagues in other HR functions such as the Organizational Development function, the Recruiting function, and/or the Compensation function.

The Meeting Scribe—Unless you are very comfortable taking notes as you also facilitate the Talent Review Meeting, you will want to identify an individual who is able to take notes throughout the meeting. This requires a specific skill set, which will be described in this section.

Executive Assistants—These individuals are instrumental in making the Talent Review Meetings happen, assisting with scheduling, facilities, and other important meeting logistics.

Business Partners—In this section we will discuss the steps that Business Leaders should take before, during and after the Talent Review Meeting to ensure the most effective process.

WORKING WITH HUMAN RESOURCE PARTNERS

To most effectively work with your HR Partners <u>BEFORE</u> the Talent Review Meeting, it will be important for you to:

- Continuously communicate the strategy, project timeline, deadlines and expectations to enable the Human Resource (HR) Partners to answer questions and carry out the action steps accurately

- Continuously thank your HR Partners for their support and time

- Ask for their help to track (and motivate) the progress of any pre-work required of the Business Leaders prior to the Talent Review Meeting

- Ask your HR Partners to fully participate in the Talent Review Meetings, and to come prepared with any applicable information about the individuals to be discussed in the meeting

<u>DURING</u> the Talent Review Meeting, the ideal role of the HR Partner is to participate fully in the meeting and add their data points, thoughts and opinions along with the Business Leaders. This is because the HR Partners often have data points and observations that others in the group will not have, and therefore they can provide a unique perspective in the meeting.

<u>AFTER</u> the Talent Review Meeting, ask the HR Partners to work with the Business Leaders to discuss development plan actions with employees, and to follow through on these development actions throughout the year.

WORKING WITH THE MEETING SCRIBE

Taking accurate and effective notes in a Talent Review Meeting is an important responsibility. The notes will serve as the basis for career and development action planning throughout the year. These notes could be called upon for legal purposes, just as performance reviews and other employee documents are subject to this potential action.

> **The Talent Review Meeting Scribe is responsible for typing all notes and decisions made during the meeting.**
>
> **The Scribe may also serve as a co-facilitator of the meeting, asking questions for clarification and additional information as needed.**

How to Select a Scribe

The Scribe's key responsibility is to ensure the accuracy and appropriateness of the data recorded from the meeting discussions. The most effective talent meeting scribes demonstrate the following competencies:

- The ability to convert discussion data into "HR appropriate" language for the meeting documents

- A strong knowledge level of the Talent Management strategy and Talent Review Meeting process to effectively capture the key discussion points

- The trust level and confidence of the meeting participants that notes are being captured accurately during the meeting, and that the data recorded will be used appropriately and in a confidential manner

- Knowledge of your organization's development resources to assist in providing action plan recommendations

You may want to ask an Organizational Development colleague to scribe the meeting—this individual can serve a dual role in the meeting by suggesting develop actions and appropriate development resources during the meeting.

Another Scribe idea to consider is to ask a Recruiting colleague to scribe the meeting. This provides an opportunity for the Recruiting Professional to hear first-hand about available talent in the organization to fill future open positions.

WORKING WITH BUSINESS LEADERS AND ASSISTANTS

Working with Business Leaders

As the Talent Management Project Lead, it is imperative that you work with Business Leaders to ensure they are prepared for the Talent Review Meeting. The diagram below describes the actions Business Leaders should take before, during and after the Talent Review Meeting:

Before the Meeting	During the Meeting	After the Meeting
Create your own succession plan and identify your high potential employees; discuss this with your own manager	Bring your employees' Talent Profiles and career interest notes to the meeting	Discuss development plan actions from the Talent Review meeting with employees as appropriate
Obtain a Talent Profile (or a current resume) from each employee	Be objective - use factual business data points when discussing talent and succession plans	Work with employees to follow through on Talent Review meeting action plans throughout the year
Talk with employees about career path ideas, relocation ability, and interest in advancing as a leader	It is important to listen to all discussions - employees from other groups may be your next top talent	Work with Human Resources to update succession plans as needed during the year
Complete a talent assessment process, and/or review past Performance Appraisals of employees	Keep the "big picture" in mind - encourage cross functional employee career movement	Use the succession plans and internal talent information to fill newly vacant positions

Working with Executive Assistants

Executive Assistants can be your best friend and partner as you implement your strategy, assisting you with:

- Coordinating the schedules of multiple leaders to identify potential dates for Talent Review Meetings—this can be a difficult challenge so it is important to work with the Executive Assistants to make this happen
- Setting up meeting logistics such as the most appropriate conference room, the catering and beverages, making copies, etc.
- Making travel arrangements for you and for the Talent Review Meeting participants if applicable

SECTION THREE
PLANNING THE TALENT REVIEW MEETING

This section provides information for the Talent Review Meeting Project Lead to design and plan for the Talent Review Meeting. A planning checklist is shown below:

- ☐ Clarify your Talent Management Business Goals

- ☐ Identify your metrics and obtain baseline data *now*

- ☐ Define your Talent Meeting scope (who will participate and who will be discussed?)

- ☐ Select Talent Review Meeting agenda items and provide this document to the Business Leaders so they will be prepared to discuss each item on the agenda

- ☐ Define your Talent Review Meeting Ground Rules

- ☐ Create definitions that meet your needs—what is a High Potential in your organization? What is a Successor in your organization?

- ☐ Schedule Talent Review Meetings with meeting participants and reserve facilities, catering, audio/visual equipment, etc. (typically this must be done months in advance in order to secure the time with senior-level leaders; one tip is to "attach" the Talent Review Meeting to another staff meeting or strategy session that is already planned for the leaders so they are only traveling once for two important meetings)

- ☐ Identify a Scribe for the meeting

- ☐ Communicate with your Human Resource partners to keep them informed and ensure they are schedule to attend the Talent Review Meetings as appropriate

- ☐ Be prepared for questions (i.e. How will successors and high potentials be developed? Who will have access to the talent information? How will the program be measured?)

DEFINING YOUR GOALS

What are your Talent Management business goals? What situation(s) have occurred to cause the interest in implementing or enhancing your Talent Management strategy? Use the worksheet on this page with the partners and sponsors of your strategy to clarify your vision and goals.

Describe your current Talent Management situation here:

Describe an ideal Talent Management state here:

What are the gaps?

What are your first-year goals?

Note: If you are launching a talent and succession management strategy for the first time in your company, remember that a primary and critical goal of the first year is simply to communicate the strategy effectively and to train everyone to execute the process, so create first-year goals that you can realistically achieve.

What are your long-term goals for your Talent Management strategy?

What baseline metrics can you gather now to help you measure your results?

DEFINING YOUR TALENT REVIEW MEETING SCOPE

One of your first decisions is determining the scope of your Talent Review Meetings—how many levels of leaders will participate in the meetings, and how many employees will be reviewed?

For example, you may want to have a short meeting with the senior leader of the group, to discuss his or her direct reports and his or her own succession plan. Your next Talent Review Meeting will be with the next line of leadership (such as a Senior Executive Vice President group) to discuss their direct reports (i.e. the Vice President talent group).

Since the organizational structure of each group or department is different, you will need to review the group's org chart to determine how many meetings are needed. An example of a "tier meeting" process that could occur over a two-day period is shown below:

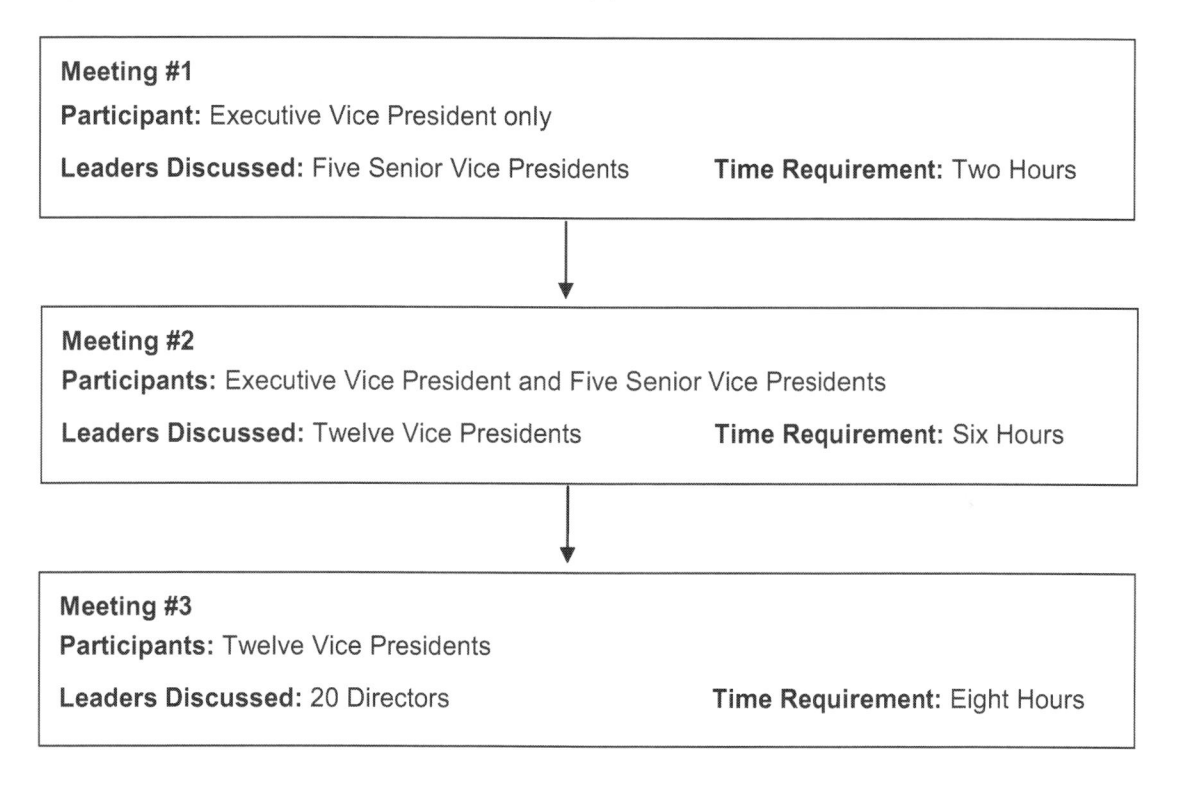

Meeting #1
Participant: Executive Vice President only
Leaders Discussed: Five Senior Vice Presidents   **Time Requirement:** Two Hours

↓

Meeting #2
Participants: Executive Vice President and Five Senior Vice Presidents
Leaders Discussed: Twelve Vice Presidents   **Time Requirement:** Six Hours

↓

Meeting #3
Participants: Twelve Vice Presidents
Leaders Discussed: 20 Directors   **Time Requirement:** Eight Hours

This example shows a "top-down" approach to the tiered Talent Review Meeting process. The advantage of this approach is that the senior leaders of the company or group begin the process by clarifying the talent needs of the organization, and by serving as a positive role model.

Another option is to reverse this order, having the supervisor or middle management level complete their Talent Review Meeting first, and then continue to *roll up* the Talent Review data into higher levels of leadership, finishing with the top senior level meeting. This will provide an opportunity for the senior leader to complete a final review of all of the decisions that have taken place during the Talent Review Meetings throughout his or her business group. The other advantage of a "roll-up" process is that talent at lower levels in the organization have already been reviewed and can now be considered for successor positions at higher levels.

DEFINING YOUR TALENT MANAGEMENT TIMELINE

Most organizations complete a full Talent Management cycle every 12 months, but this timeline varies based on organizational needs, size and scope. During the planning process, define your timeline, monthly or quarterly milestones, and create a project action plan.

A high-level basic Talent Management process cycle is shown below:

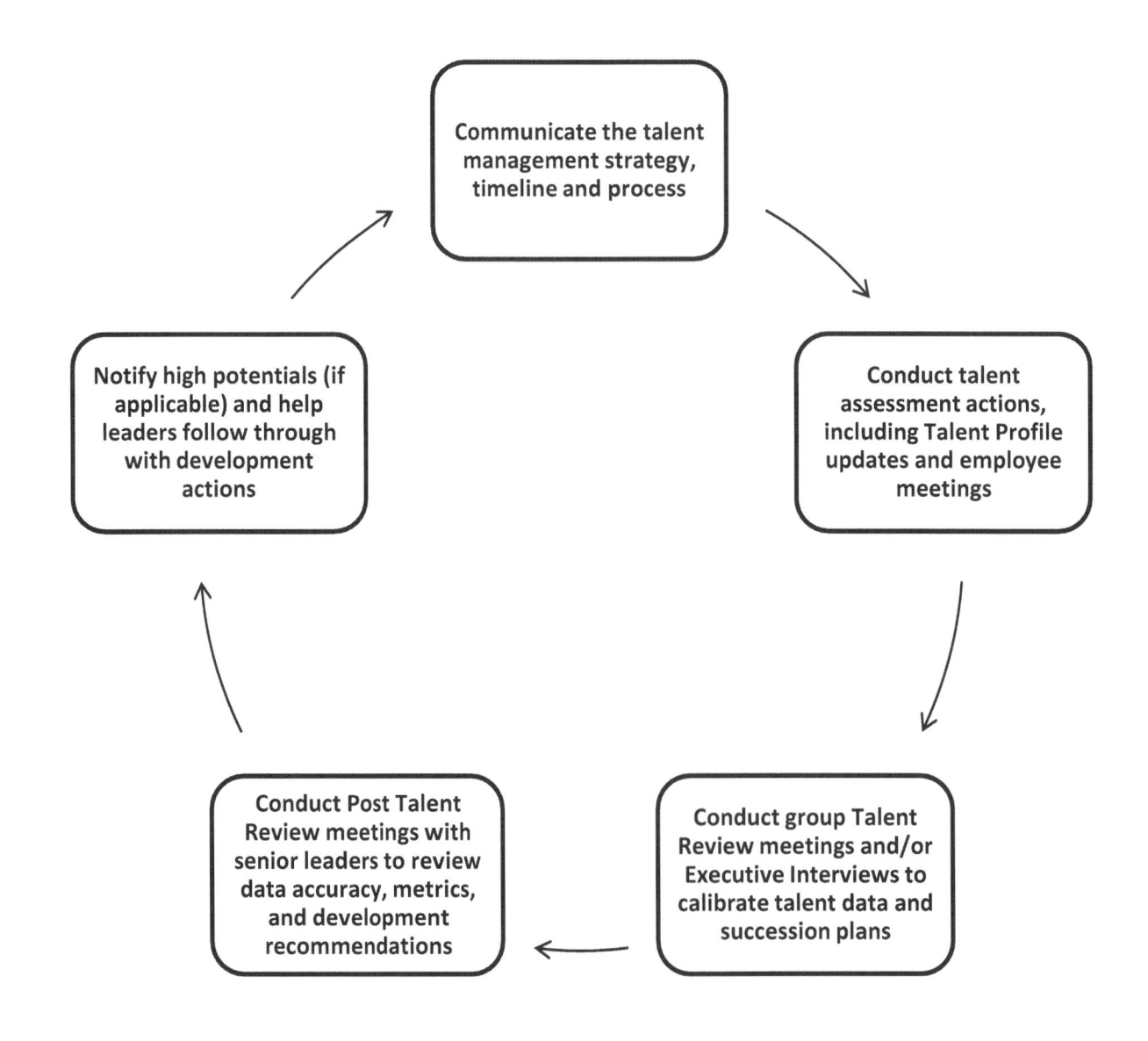

- Communicate the talent management strategy, timeline and process
- Conduct talent assessment actions, including Talent Profile updates and employee meetings
- Conduct group Talent Review meetings and/or Executive Interviews to calibrate talent data and succession plans
- Conduct Post Talent Review meetings with senior leaders to review data accuracy, metrics, and development recommendations
- Notify high potentials (if applicable) and help leaders follow through with development actions

A SAMPLE ANNUAL TALENT REVIEW TIMELINE

If you are putting together a timeline for your annual talent review process, you may be wondering how much time each step of the process will take. A <u>sample</u> timeline (based on a calendar year project plan) is shown below to assist you as you create a timeline for your own company.

1st Quarter

- Business leaders conduct performance review meetings (and career discussions) with employees
- The Talent Review Project Lead updates the Human Resources team on the current talent management strategy, processes, deadline dates, etc. to ensure they are ready to support the business leaders
- The Talent Review Project Lead (and/or the HR Team) executes the communication plans to prepare business leaders to begin the Talent Review process

2nd Quarter

- The Talent Review Project lead schedules and facilitates Talent Review Meetings for all designated levels and/or departments to calibrate talent information, succession plans, high potential employees, and development actions

3rd Quarter

- Conduct evaluation surveys with participants of the Talent Review process to identify strengths and improvement areas of the Talent Review meetings (just as you would after conducting a workshop)
- Analyze the data from all Talent Review Meetings; identify themes, trends and overall development recommendations; develop presentations and/or reports to communicate results to senior leaders
- Work with managers and employees to follow through on development actions as identified in the Talent Review Meetings; if applicable, notify high potential leaders to begin development

4th Quarter

- Use the evalation survey data (and/or interviews with participants of the Talent Review process) to form ideas for improvements to the Talent Review process; update the strategy and procedures for the coming year and update communication materials accordingly
- Continue to work with high potentials and business leaders to follow through on development plans
- Measure results and keep talent data updated on your system or talent data tracking spreadsheets

A SAMPLE MULTI-YEAR TALENT MANAGEMENT PLAN

Typically an organization will implement a talent and succession management process in phases over multiple years (unless the organization is lucky enough to have an entire team to plan and execute the strategy and to facilitate multiple Talent Review Meetings within 1-2 years).

As the Talent Review Project Lead, you may want to consider an initial plan to implement a talent management process within a specific "layer" of the organization (such as starting with the executive team only), or within a specific department (such as implementing the process with a pilot group in the organization). This enables you to plan and "fine-tune" your process before implementing the strategy throughout the entire company. It also can provide an opportunity to measure results, comparing metrics within the pilot group to metrics within comparison groups.

What can you expect to accomplish each year as you continue to implement and enhance your talent management strategy over the first three years?

Year of Implementation	Key Milestones and Accomplishments
Year One	• In the first year, leaders learn how to talk about performance of their people with others, how to identify and assess talent, and how to prepare for and participate in a Talent Review Meeting • Form a Talent Management Strategy in conjunction with Business Leaders • Plan and prepare resources and processes that will be used to develop leaders, successors and high potentials identified in the Talent Review Meetings • Identify metrics and obtain baseline data • Create talent assessment tools and communication materials for leaders • Execute a Talent Review process with one level of leadership and/or with a pilot group • Follow-through with Talent Review Meeting data, recommendations, and actions
Year Two	• In the second year, accountability is increased as leaders and employees work with HR to follow through on Talent Review action items (as the progress and results from action items identified in Year 1 will be discussed this year) • Expand the Talent Review process to additional levels of leaders and/or in additional departments of the organization • Enhance your strategy and processes as needed based on feedback from Year 1 • Expand resources to develop leaders, successors and high potentials • Measure your first year results, comparing current metrics to your baseline metrics
Year Three	• Now the Talent Review process should be well-understood by leaders and the strategy is becoming part of your culture • Continue to expand the program as you have the people, resources and budget to support it

IDENTIFY YOUR TALENT MEETING DISCUSSION TOPICS

Another important decision is to identify the agenda items you will focus on in the Talent Review Meeting. As the Talent Management Project Lead, you will want to identify this early in the planning process so you can communicate the agenda items to the Business Leaders; this enables them to include the correct discussion items in their 1-on-1 meetings with employees prior to the Talent Review Meeting. This section discusses typical agenda items to consider for your meeting:

Review the Talent Profile—Start the discussion of each individual by a <u>brief</u> review of his or her Talent Profile. The purpose of this discussion is to ensure everyone is aware of the candidate's education, previous work experience, competencies, etc. This profile discussion should take approximately one minute; it is a good idea to have the facilitator present this quick profile review, because the Business Leader is more likely to spend considerable time on the profile, which can take away from the important career and development discussions.

Discuss Position Vacancy Risk—Discuss the likelihood that the individual will leave the organization within the next 12 months. Amazingly, managers are often quite aware of the vacancy risk of their direct reports. To expedite the discussion, provide some qualifying terms for the leaders to use. For example, ask, "What is the likelihood that this individual will leave the organization over the next 12 months—is it high, moderate or low?"

Then, it is important to discuss the reason for the vacancy risk and the impact to the organization if the individual leaves. Depending on the outcome of that discussion, discuss the next action plan that is appropriate. **Imagine the difference in the action plans for the following two high-risk vacancy risk discussions:**

Vacancy Risk	Reason	Business Impact	Action Plan
High	Marketable skill set and a strong networker	High—Monica is the account manager for our top client	Retention Succession Plan
High	Dissatisfied with the company	Low—Jenna's performance has affected by her dissatisfaction with the company	Coaching Performance Plan

Leadership Experience and Competencies—Discuss the scope of the individual's previous leadership experience and his or her competencies in the areas of coaching, strategic planning, identifying talent, business acumen, developing people, addressing performance issues, etc.

Overall Strengths—Discuss other performance strengths and special talents of the individual.

TALENT MEETING DISCUSSION TOPICS (CONTINUED)

Overall Development Areas—Discuss competency gaps and areas of weakness or development.

Potential Successors of the Individual—Discuss other candidates who could fill the individual's position, including a quick review of any competency gaps to be developed to increase the candidates' readiness and qualifications.

Potential Succession Positions—Discuss positions the individual could potentially move into as a successor.

Short Term Career Potential—Discuss potential short-term career paths that would be applicable over the next 1-2 years.

Long Term Career Potential—Discuss potential long-term career paths that would be applicable over the next 2+ years.

Identify High Potential Talent—Discuss and agree upon the selection of high potential individuals, based on the discussion of leadership ability, strengths, career path ideas, etc.

Formal Development Actions—Identify workshops, books, e-learning, degree programs, conferences, industry associations, etc. that address to the individual's development needs.

On-the-Job Development Actions—Identify projects, job assignments, job rotations, new roles and responsibilities that would help the individual leverage strengths and address development needs.

Other Actions—Identify other actions that address issues that surfaced during the Talent Review Meeting discussions, such as reviewing an individual's compensation, scheduling a coaching discussion with the employee, etc.

Create a Notes Tool

Once you identify your Talent Review Meeting agenda items, create a document or spreadsheet with each agenda item and a blank box for the Scribe to enter notes pertaining to that item (unless you have a talent management online system to document your Talent Review Meeting notes). An example of this type of simple Scribe Notes Tool is shown on page 86 of this book.

SAMPLE TALENT MEETING AGENDA

Each Talent Review Meeting throughout the organization should include consistent elements. A sample Talent Review Meeting Agenda is shown below:

Basic Sample Talent Review Meeting Agenda

Time	Item
10 minutes	**Welcome: Introductions, Objectives, Agenda**
15 minutes	**Business Goals, Talent and Competency Needs**
10 minutes	**Review Ground Rules**
15 minutes per individual	**Leadership Review of Talent and Career Potential** - Display and Discuss Talent Profile Information - Review Vacancy Risk, Reasons and Action Plans - Discuss Strengths and Development Areas - Determine Career and Development Actions - Discuss Leadership Abilities - Finalize and Document Action Plans
1 hour	**Succession Plan Discussion and finalization of High Potential selections**
15 minutes	**Wrap Up** - How to use this information – confidentiality issues - Next steps – follow up discussions

SAMPLE MEETING GROUND RULES

Discussing "Ground Rules" at the beginning of a Talent Review Meeting helps to ensure that talent discussions focus on business behaviors and results, and increases the effectiveness of the discussions. Create a Ground Rules document to distribute in the meeting, or discuss Ground Rules and document on a flip chart during the meeting.

SAMPLE TALENT REVIEW MEETING GROUND RULES

- ☑ **Use *factual* data points – what was observed, what was heard, and what were the business results?**

- ☑ **Use *recent* data points – behaviors and results which occurred in approximately the last year**

- ☑ **Use appropriate references, avoiding references to age, family status, personal life situations, etc.**

- ☑ **Focus on development and building future leadership benchstrength**

- ☑ **Listen to all discussions, especially the individuals you may not know**

- ☑ **Remember that these discussions represent a "snapshot in time" – people change**

- ☑ **Think about what is best for the whole organization**

- ☑ **Listen – avoid interruptions**

- ☑ **Stay on track and keep data points focused**

- ☑ **Consider both current leadership needs and future leadership needs**

- ☑ **Use the information on a "confidential, need to know" basis**

- ☑ **Keep cell phones, and other electronic devices on vibrate**

DEFINITIONS: WHAT IS A HIGH POTENTIAL?

Another step in the Talent Review planning process is to develop clear definitions of high potentials and successors. There are many ways to define a high potential, so you will need to identify the criteria that makes sense for your organization. For example, the ability to relocate may be a critical characteristic of a high potential employee in a large, global organization but may not be applicable at all in a smaller, local organization.

Reference the charts below describing the high potential traits of **ASPIRATION** and the **ABILITY** as you create your own definition of a high potential employee:

Aspiration	Ability
Desires leadership advancement	Has the ability to advance or move laterally rapidly into significant and complex leadership roles
Is open to career movement, challenging roles and/or relocation	Demonstrates high learning agility, creativity and strategic thinking skills
Is willing to move laterally to increase breadth of skills	Is able to work in an ambiguous and rapidly changing environment
Seeks and acts on feedback for continuous improvement	Demonstrates superior interpersonal skills and is respected by others
Follows through with learning assignments and development actions	Effectively deals with stress, organizational politics and emotions
Is self-motivated and highly engaged in the organization	Leverages strengths and develops (or compensates for) weaknesses

DEFINITIONS: WHAT IS A SUCCESSOR?

Another key to an effective Talent Review process is to identify the levels and types of successors that are applicable to your organization, and to distribute clear definitions of each successor category.

Succession Planning typically identifies:

- Successors for specific replacement positions
- Talent pools for positions with similar competencies
- Competency gaps that must be addressed to develop future successors into prepared successors

You will need to form definitions for leaders to identify successors in a consistent fashion. Some sample definitions are shown below.

Successor Definitions

Prepared or Qualified Successors – Employees who currently possess and demonstrate all of the required qualifications for the incumbent's position.

This does not mean that a candidate who is ready today for the position has EVERY competency that the incumbent leader demonstrates, but they must have the required competencies and the potential to obtain the additional preferred competencies for the position.

To help leaders identify prepared successors, ask the question, "If the position were open today, which employees in the company would you consider to be qualified to interview for the position now?"

Future Successors – Employees who are not currently qualified for the incumbent's position but could develop the required competencies, education, and/or work experience within an approximate 1-2 year timeframe should be identified for this successor category.

Pipeline Candidates – Employees who are not currently qualified but could develop the required competencies, education, and/or work experience within an approximate 3-5 year timeframe should be identified for this successor category.

Emergency Candidates – Some organizations identify someone (or multiple persons) who will handle the position on a temporary basis until either the incumbent returns from a leave of absence or until the position is filled.

DEFINITIONS: WHAT IS A KEY EXPERT?

In addition to identifying high potentials and successors, some organizations also identify employees who are key experts.

Defined as individual contributors (or leaders) who have achieved a distinguished level of expertise in their field, key experts contribute in significant and unique ways in the organization, but they may not demonstrate the desire or ability to advance quickly into new leadership roles.

The unique competency set of a key expert (which should include extensive knowledge and experience within the company as well as specialized skill sets and qualifications) would be nearly impossible to replace if the individual left the organization. For this reason, key experts should identify and develop successors just as leaders do, and they should provide training and serve in mentor roles to others within the organization.

> The primary purpose of a Key Expert program is to **RECOGNIZE** and **RETAIN** employees who prefer to pursue a career track of significant expertise rather than focusing on significant advancement in a leadership track.

Many key experts also serve on external boards and committees that influence their industry, and they may publish papers and serve as speakers to provide more positive visibility and publicity for their company. Other key experts may create new products and services for the organization, or they may be the top employees managing the accounts of key customers for the company.

Organizations that identify key experts typically provide stock options or other compensation retention packages to these individuals. Organizations with a key expert identification strategy typically have a significant population of employees who are highly educated, qualified and specialized in their field.

BEGIN TO DESIGN A DEVELOPMENT PROGRAM NOW

If your talent management strategy includes the identification of high potential employees, **now** is the time to begin to plan and design development resources or a curriculum for these employees. It takes time to design the objectives and content of the high potential program, and time to either work with vendors or to create the development activities and courses. You will also need time to define and obtain the budget for your high potential curriculum, so if you wait to design the development program after your First Talent Review Meeting process, there will be a significant delay in your implementation timeline (and in your business results from the program).

There are two key reasons it is important to begin the design of a high potential program during the initial Talent Review Meeting planning phase:

- The development program for high potential employees can be developed as you continue to plan and roll out the Talent Review process, so the program will be ready after the completion of the meetings
- You will want to be prepared to answer questions from Business Leaders during the Talent Review Meetings such as, "How are we going to develop these high potential employees after we identify them?"

Consider a wide variety of both on-the-job development actions and formal training resources to develop your high potential employees. Use the questions below to help plan your high potential development strategy:

1. Who will take the lead for developing high potential employees (i.e. the managers of the high potential employees, the Learning and Development department, etc.)?

2. What budget resources do we have for the program (or, what funding will we need to obtain?)

3. Will each high potential employee stay in the development program for a specific period of time, or will each individual continue in the program until the Business Leaders decide to move him or her out of the program during the Talent Review Meeting process?

4. How will we use our organization's Leadership Competencies (or Values) in the program?

5. What will be the involvement level of our Business Executives in the program?

6. How will the development program be evaluated? How will we know if the program is achieving the business results of our overall Talent Management Strategy?

7. Will we have different programs for high potentials at different levels in the organization (i.e. an Emerging High Potential program and an Executive High Potential program)?

8. Will our development program include job rotations and/or new job assignments?

PLANNING THE LENGTH AND LOGISTICS OF THE MEETING

The length of each Talent Review Meeting will vary considerably, and as the HR partner, you will need to assist your Business Leaders to plan an appropriate amount of time to schedule for each Talent Review Meeting.

Multiple factors will affect the timing of the Talent Review Meeting:

- The **number of individuals to be discussed** during the meeting

- The **number of components or agenda items** you want to include in your Talent Review Meeting

- The **communication style of the meeting participants** (and especially the communication style of the senior leader of the group)

- The **number of meeting attendees** (the more attendees, the more time you will need)

- The **previous experience** the leaders have in participating in a Talent Review Meeting (if this is their first meeting, more time will be needed)

Of course you will also need to factor in time for breaks and for lunch, if applicable. Build in enough time for breaks to enable leaders to check their e-mail and voice mail. If the leaders' tolerance level allows, it is ideal to be able to schedule a cushion of time (or to leave the meeting ending time open) to make sure you will be able to finish the meeting topics, *especially if meeting attendees must travel to participate in the session.*

Be sure to find out the flight arrangements of the participants, because they will leave when they need to in order to catch their flight, so it is best to know up front what your actual meeting schedule will be. If you are traveling in to attend or to facilitate the meeting, **schedule your return flight for the next morning following the meeting**. Then, if the meeting runs longer than scheduled, you will be able to stay to lead or support the meeting.

Keep in mind that the Talent Review Meeting may be one of the few times the leadership team gets together face-to-face, and many groups also like to build in team-building activities or a dinner before or after their Talent Review session. **If there is a choice, schedule time for participants to have any team-building events or dinners before the Talent Review session**, as they will typically be tired after the meeting. This strategy also provides a time for them to "catch up", socialize, and talk, to reduce this activity during the Talent Review Meeting.

CALCULATING THE LENGTH OF THE MEETING

Use the "rule of thumb" of allowing for an average of 15 minutes of discussion time for each individual discussed in a Talent Review meeting, plus time for additional discussions for the entire group, such as a review of the department's succession plans. Here is an example of the timing of a sample Talent Review Meeting:

15 Minutes	Introductions, Agenda, Ground Rules
15-30 Minutes	Senior Leader presentation of the group's business goals, the talent needs to achieve the goals, and any current and future leadership positions
3 Hours	Review the vacancy risks, strengths, development needs, career potential of 12 leaders (15 minutes each leader X 12 leaders = 180 minutes or 3 hours)
1 Hour	Reviewing nominated high potentials or top talent
1 Hour	Finalization of the group's Succession Plans (this timing of 1 hour will vary based on the number of leaders on the Succession Plan)
1 Hour	Remember to account for time that will be needed for breaks and lunch during the day
15 Minutes	Wrap up—discuss next steps and action plans
Total Meeting Time: 6.5+ Hours	

This sample Talent Review Meeting should be scheduled as an all day meeting, with flexibility around the starting and ending times depending on the group culture, flight schedule needs, etc.

This also allows some "cushion" for additional people issues that tend to come up during the meeting, and for breaks that tend to run over time as the meeting participants are returning calls, etc. And of course, if you add additional agenda items to your Talent Review Meetings, be sure to add time to your meeting to discuss these items.

CASE EXAMPLE: PLANNING A TALENT REVIEW MEETING

Read the scenario and form your Talent Review Meeting plan for this group on the next page.

Case Example: You have been asked to plan and facilitate a Talent Review Meeting for the company's Sales organization. The group's high-level organizational chart is shown below. The group has asked for a Talent Review Meeting to be completed in 3 hours, and they would like to discuss the career and development needs of the 20 Director-level leaders (not shown on the chart below) who report up to all of the SVP leaders, review their Succession Plans at the VP level, and discuss 5 individuals who have been nominated for the organization's high potential leadership program.

All 20 Directors are sales and account management leaders who report directly to the VP leaders. Ginger Thomas has asked to participate in the meeting remotely. All of the leaders in this organization have participated in at least one Talent Review Meeting, with the exception of Ginger Thomas, who is participating in a Talent Review Meeting for the first time.

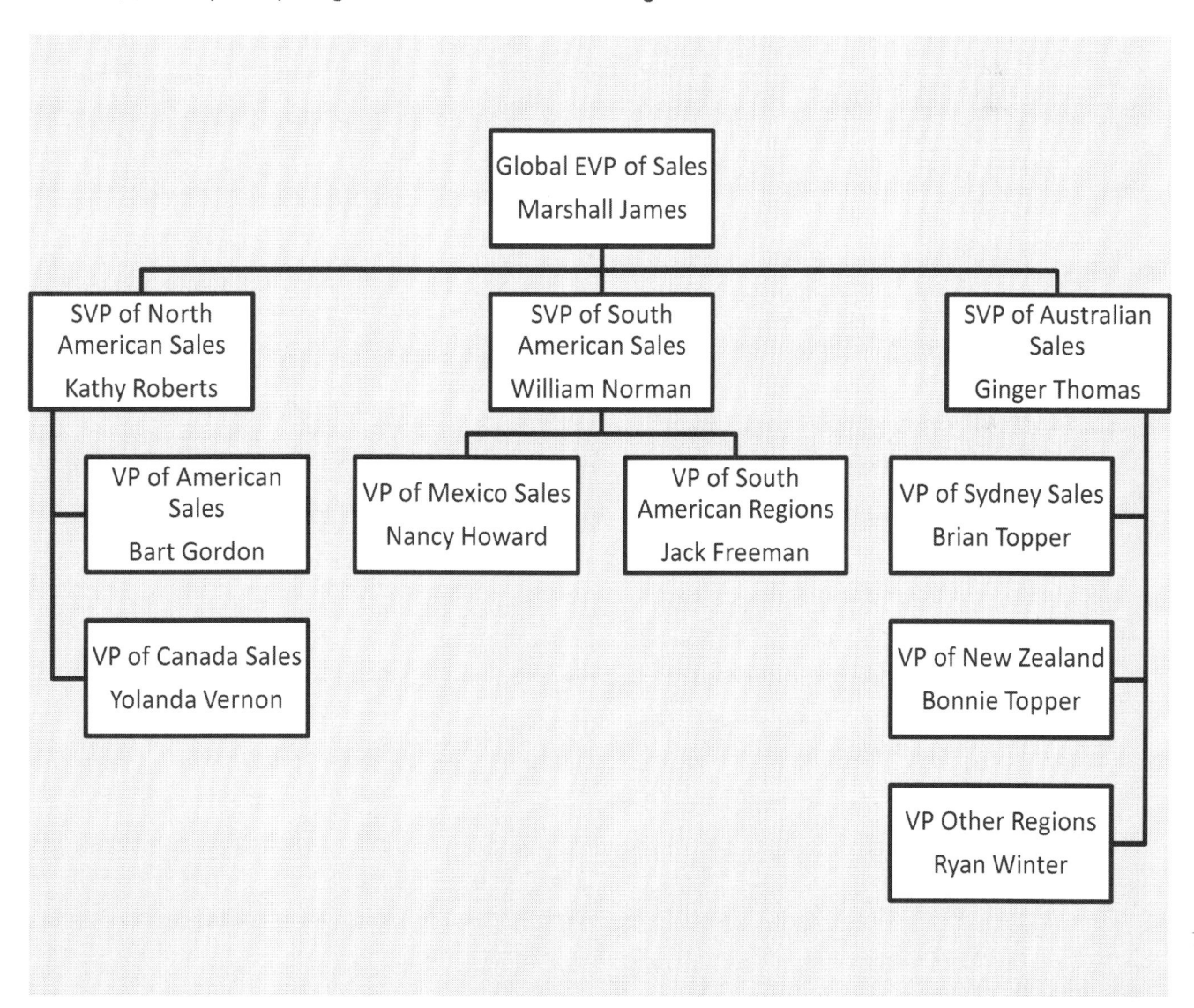

```
                    Global EVP of Sales
                      Marshall James
    ┌───────────────────────┼───────────────────────┐
SVP of North           SVP of South            SVP of Australian
American Sales         American Sales              Sales
Kathy Roberts          William Norman          Ginger Thomas
    │                   ┌───┴───┐                   │
    ├── VP of American   VP of Mexico   VP of South  ├── VP of Sydney Sales
    │   Sales            Sales          American       Brian Topper
    │   Bart Gordon      Nancy Howard   Regions       
    │                                   Jack Freeman  ├── VP of New Zealand
    └── VP of Canada Sales                            │   Bonnie Topper
        Yolanda Vernon                                │
                                                      └── VP Other Regions
                                                          Ryan Winter
```

CASE EXAMPLE WORKSHEET

Answer the following questions, and form an agenda and timing for the meeting below:

1. How many Talent Review Meetings will be needed for this group?

2. How will you handle the participant who wants to participate in the meeting virtually?

3. What might be some special considerations for this group that could affect the timing or effectiveness of the meeting, and what action(s) could you take as the facilitator to address these issues?

4. Enter the agenda and timing for a Talent Review Meeting to meet this group's needs below:

Timing	Agenda Item - Description

Total Meeting Time: _____ Hours

See sample responses to this exercise in the Appendix of this book.

A FACILITATOR PREPARATION CHECKLIST

Each year (after your strategy, process and tools are updated and finalized) use the table below as a checklist to prepare for each Talent Review Meeting:

At least 3 months prior to the Talent Review Meeting	○ Review each group's organizational chart and identify the appropriate number of meetings required, the attendees for each meeting, and the timing of each meeting ○ Meet with your internal partners (or Talent Steering Committee) to finalize all plans, and to ensure the project team has all of the information and tools they need ○ Launch your communication plans—provide training, tools, definitions and "next steps" to the business leaders who will be participating in the process
At least 2 months prior to the Talent Review Meeting	○ Work with leaders and assistants to schedule and confirm meeting dates ○ Reserve the meeting room location and obtain A/V equipment, food, etc. ○ Meet with each Senior Leader to discuss his or her role in the Talent Review Meeting ○ Provide the Meeting Agenda to the leaders who are participating in the Talent Review meetings, so they will know what they should be ready to discuss about each employee in the meeting ○ Track progress of the preparation process (i.e. are employees updating Talent Profiles, are leaders updating succession plans, meeting with employees, etc.?) ○ Make sure all travel arrangements are finalized, if applicable ○ Identify the Scribes who will be taking notes in your meetings to ensure they have the meeting dates reserved and they are prepared for their role
Approximately 2-3 weeks prior to the Talent Review Meeting	○ Follow up with leaders who have not yet completed meeting preparation actions ○ Compile the talent assessment data, 9-box data, and/or draft succession data you have requested from the business leaders prior to the meeting (or review this information on your talent management system by function or department) ○ Make sure you will have Internet access in the meeting room if you will be displaying data from an online talent management system in the meeting
Approximately 1 week prior to the Talent Review Meeting	○ Create a checklist of the names of all participants who will be discussed in the meeting—make a copy for each leader participating in the meeting ○ Make sure you have updated Talent Profiles for each employee who will discussed in the meeting—create hardcopies of these if desired for each participant (or just plan to project the profiles on a screen for viewing) ○ Make copies of the Agenda, Definitions and Ground Rules for each meeting participant (use colored paper so you can easily reference these sheets during the meeting) or create Wall Charts with this information for display in the room ○ Review all available information about the employees to be discussed in the meeting—write notes on your own materials about any questions you have about the employee

SECTION FOUR
TALENT ASSESSMENT AND PREPARATION

This section provides information for the Talent Review Meeting Project Lead to identify talent assessment tools, communicate the talent management strategy and processes, and ensure everyone is prepared for the Talent Review Meeting. A preparation checklist is shown below:

- ❏ Identify talent assessment tools (i.e. Talent Profiles, 9-Box Chart, Performance Reviews, Leadership Competency Ratings, Position Competency Models, Definitions, Meetings with Employees, Draft Succession Plans)

- ❏ Prepare your communication plan for Business Leaders—create presentations and materials

- ❏ Ask the senior leader to be prepared to discuss the business goals and talent needs at the beginning of the meeting

- ❏ Send reminders to meeting participants and monitor progress of talent assessment actions

- ❏ Create and make copies of the documents you will need for the meeting (i.e. the Talent Review Meeting Agenda, Ground Rules, Definitions, Notes Spreadsheet, etc.

- ❏ Obtain Talent Profiles or Resumes of all individuals to be discussed – plan to either display the profiles or create a booklet for meeting participants

TALENT ASSESSMENT TOOLS

Each organization will need to determine how they define and identify their top talent in the organization. A best practice talent assessment process includes:

1. A measurement of an individual's **PAST PERFORMANCE**.

2. A projection of an individual's **FUTURE POTENTIAL**.

3. Obtaining career and development needs and interests from **THE EMPLOYEE**.

Use the worksheet below to document the criteria you will use in your own organization:

What criteria can we use to measure past performance?
(Potential criteria includes past performance appraisals, leadership competency ratings, business results, past career progression, etc.)

What criteria can we use to project future potential?
(Potential criteria includes learning agility ratings/assessments, projected leadership ability ratings, desire for career movement, desire for leadership advancement, relocation ability, job competency models, etc.)

What actions can we take to provide support and structure for managers to meet with employees to discuss career interests, relocation ability, and development needs?
(For example, employees can create or update their own Talent Profile, and managers can use the Career Discussion tool on the following page to assist with employee discussions.)

A TOOL FOR MANAGERS: EMPLOYEE CAREER DISCUSSIONS

The questions shown below can be used to create a "Talking Points" tool for managers to have a career and development discussion with each employee prior to the Talent Review Meeting. This discussion is critical for an effective Talent Review Meeting.

If these employee discussions don't take place, you may receive "I don't know" answers to questions like this: "To be a successor for this position, Marci would need to be able to relocate—is she willing to relocate?" "Does Marci want to move into a management position?" And when you receive a lot of "I don't know" answers to these types of questions, it is very difficult to build valid succession plans and to identify high potentials for new leadership positions.

Manager – Employee Career Discussion Tool

Prior to the Talent Review Meeting:

1. Ask each employee to either update their Talent Profile or to provide an updated Resume.

2. Begin the meeting with a discussion of the Talent Profile to refresh your memory on the employee's past work experience, education, qualifications, etc. Let the employee know that the company is beginning the annual talent planning process to discuss potential career paths and development actions for employees, and part of that process is for managers to meet with employees to discuss own career and development interests.

3. Discuss the following with each employee:

    a. What do you enjoy most about your current position?

    b. What do you enjoy least about your current position?

    c. Think about a time that you most enjoyed your job and you felt you contributed at a very high level—what was it about that job that created this "best case" career scenario?

    d. How would you describe your satisfaction and enjoyment of your current position?

    e. What career path opportunities and ideas are you most interested in? Consider positions both within our department/division and those in other functional areas.

    f. Are there potential career paths that would never be of interest to you and/or they would not be a good fit for your talents, abilities and interests?

    g. What interests you most about these potential career paths?

    h. What abilities and value could you contribute in these potential positions?

    i. What work experiences, education, and/or qualifications do you think you would you need in order to be qualified for these potential positions?

    j. What projects or new job responsibilities would you potentially be interested in?

    k. What development opportunities and/or training would you be interested in, and how would this contribute to your current and future performance?

    l. Are you interested in moving into (or staying in) a leadership position and managing a staff of direct and/or indirect reports?

    m. What is your ability to relocate, both now and in the future? Are there areas you would or would not move to, or are you open to any location?

    n. Are you interested in a global job assignment? (If applicable)

    o. Is there anything else you would like to add about your career and development interests?

CONSISTENCY IS KEY

Within the three best practice categories of talent assessment discussed on page 58 (reviewing past performance, estimating future potential, and meeting with employees), it is critical to remember that your talent assessment criteria, definitions, processes and tools are used CONSISTENTLY throughout the organization.

Why is this important? You want to make sure your talent assessment process is fair, valid, and legally defensible. All employees who are involved in and/or reviewed each year should be measured against the same criteria.

> Talent Management pertains to your **internal recruiting tools and processes**; therefore, it is subject to external audit and review just as your **external recruiting tools and processes** are subject to audit and review. A good rule of thumb is: "If the tool or action you are considering would not be fair and appropriate for external recruiting, then don't use it for your internal talent management process."
>
> Talent management always requires a balancing act between 1) customizing to the business needs of the various managers in the organization, and 2) ensuring that processes and tools are centrally created to ensure a fair and consistent process.
>
> For example, what if managers in an organization all created and used their own job application forms for external candidates applying for open positions? This might have the advantage of customizing the application form to specific business functional needs, but the disadvantage of having inconsistent job application forms within the same organization, which subjects the organization to potential litigation overrides the customization advantage. Therefore, all organizations use one job application form throughout the organization.

Your Talent Management processes and tools are subject to external audits and your talent data is discoverable information in the event of litigation. Therefore, it is important that criteria is used for talent selection (not simply the opinions of the leaders) and that all processes and talent data are...

- **Consistently applied**
- **Documented**
- **Written in HR appropriate terms**

DEFINING TALENT ASSESSMENT TOOLS

Another decision to make during the Talent Review Meeting planning process is, "What talent assessment tools will we use?" Remember in this first phase of the Talent Management process, you are gathering information regarding past performance, future potential and employee desires.

The chart below defines four of the most-commonly used talent assessment tools:

Tool Definition	How is it Used?
Talent Profile—An internal resume that provides a snapshot of an individual's qualifications and talents. Typically a Talent Profile is designed to fit on one page to ensure a concise "picture" of the individual.	**Before the meeting:** Either the manager or the employee updates their Talent Profile with current information. **During the meeting:** Talent Profiles can either be projected on a screen during the Talent Review Meeting, or a booklet of Talent Profiles can be distributed to participants during (and/or before) the meeting. **After the meeting:** Current Talent Profiles can be stored and viewed online, or hardcopy versions may be centrally maintained and stored.
The 9-Box Chart—A table that displays a cross-reference of each employee's performance and potential.	**Before the meeting:** Either the Business Leaders or the Human Resource Professionals may gather performance and potential numeric ratings and plot these on the chart for a visual reference. **During the meeting:** The pre-plotted chart may be distributed or displayed. Some organizations use a 9-box chart on a flip chart during the meeting and use "sticky notes" to make changes based on discussions. **After the meeting:** A finalized 9-box chart with plot points (rather than names) may be used after the Talent Review Meeting as a way to view the leadership benchstrength at a high level. These charts can be compared between functional areas and from year to year to observe trends.
Leadership Competency Rating Systems—An organization may create a spreadsheet or online rating system to measure leadership behaviors for each individual.	**Before the meeting:** Managers enter their ratings in the competency assessment tool provided. The Talent Management Project Lead gathers and reviews this information prior to the meeting. **During the meeting:** Ratings may be referenced during the discussions and used to identify strengths, development needs and actions. **After the meeting:** Leadership ratings may be placed on Talent Profiles or an online talent management system to provide "snapshot" information.
Position Competency Models—A competency chart that defines the knowledge, skills and abilities that lead to high performance in a specific position or in a job family.	**Before the meeting:** Managers and Human Resource Professionals (and often external consultants) work together to identify the high performance competencies required for the job position or family to create the models. **During the meeting:** Position competency models may be distributed or displayed during the meeting for reference during career path discussions. **After the meeting:** Competency models are most effectively used online for employees to access, enabling them to compare their current competencies and qualifications to the competencies required for positions of interest.

TALENT ASSESSMENT TOOLS: THE TALENT PROFILE

The Talent Profile typically contains this basic information:

- Name / General Information
- Hire Date / Last Position Movement / Work Experience
- Education / Certifications / Licenses
- Special Skills, Accomplishments, Awards, Languages
- Career Interests / Relocation Ability

Most executives will want a 1-page Talent Profile, so plan for that from the beginning!

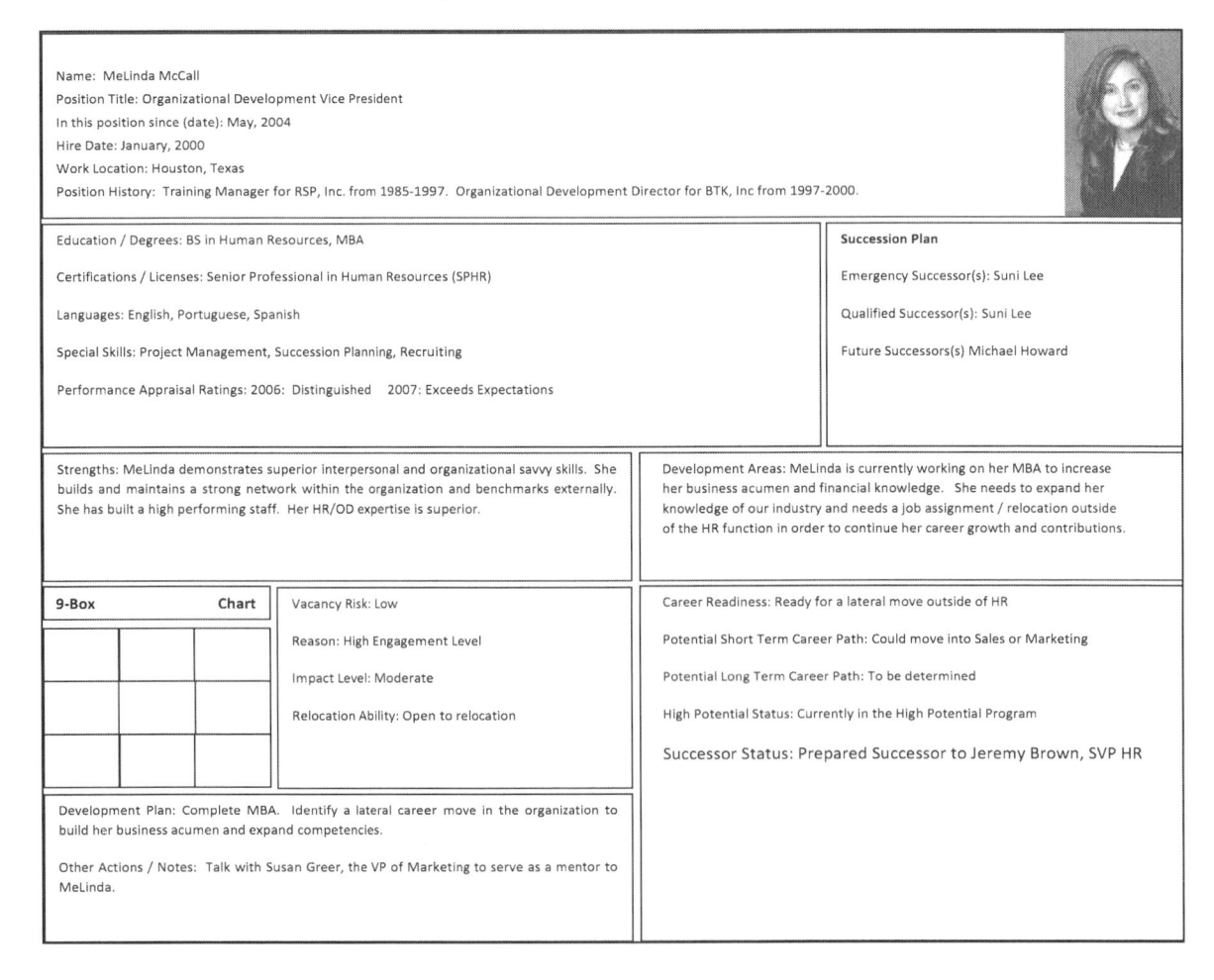

Name: MeLinda McCall
Position Title: Organizational Development Vice President
In this position since (date): May, 2004
Hire Date: January, 2000
Work Location: Houston, Texas
Position History: Training Manager for RSP, Inc. from 1985-1997. Organizational Development Director for BTK, Inc from 1997-2000.

Education / Degrees: BS in Human Resources, MBA	**Succession Plan**
Certifications / Licenses: Senior Professional in Human Resources (SPHR)	Emergency Successor(s): Suni Lee
Languages: English, Portuguese, Spanish	Qualified Successor(s): Suni Lee
Special Skills: Project Management, Succession Planning, Recruiting	Future Successors(s) Michael Howard
Performance Appraisal Ratings: 2006: Distinguished 2007: Exceeds Expectations	

Strengths: MeLinda demonstrates superior interpersonal and organizational savvy skills. She builds and maintains a strong network within the organization and benchmarks externally. She has built a high performing staff. Her HR/OD expertise is superior.

Development Areas: MeLinda is currently working on her MBA to increase her business acumen and financial knowledge. She needs to expand her knowledge of our industry and needs a job assignment / relocation outside of the HR function in order to continue her career growth and contributions.

9-Box Chart		
	Vacancy Risk: Low	Career Readiness: Ready for a lateral move outside of HR
	Reason: High Engagement Level	Potential Short Term Career Path: Could move into Sales or Marketing
	Impact Level: Moderate	Potential Long Term Career Path: To be determined
	Relocation Ability: Open to relocation	High Potential Status: Currently in the High Potential Program
		Successor Status: Prepared Successor to Jeremy Brown, SVP HR

Development Plan: Complete MBA. Identify a lateral career move in the organization to build her business acumen and expand competencies.

Other Actions / Notes: Talk with Susan Greer, the VP of Marketing to serve as a mentor to MeLinda.

Should a photo be posted on the profile? There is no one "right answer" to the question concerning photos on a Talent Profile. Those who favor having the photo on the profile point out that it is important to make sure that everyone is discussing the same individual—especially if the organization is large enough to have employees with identical names. And, photos can increase the visibility of talent in the organization and assist managers in connecting "names with faces". Those who favor profiles without photos point out that photos would never be used on external resumes due to the potential for discrimination and for assumptions to be formed about an individual. Each organization must make a decision that best meets their business needs, size, and culture.

THE 9-BOX CHART

The 9-box chart has been emerging as a Talent Management best practice tool. It may also be a 6-box chart, a 12-box chart, etc. depending on the organization's needs.

The most important things to remember about the 9-box chart are:

1. It should be backed by criteria – how are you measuring that performance and potential?

2. It is a snapshot in time and can change from year to year.

3. Just because an individual "lands" in the top talent box does not mean you should automatically identify/notify them as a high potential.

4. Just because an individual "lands" in the low performance and potential box does not mean he or she should be placed on probation or terminated. Individuals may be in this box temporarily when they are learning a new position in the company.

5. Some organizations place descriptors in each box to assist managers with the process.

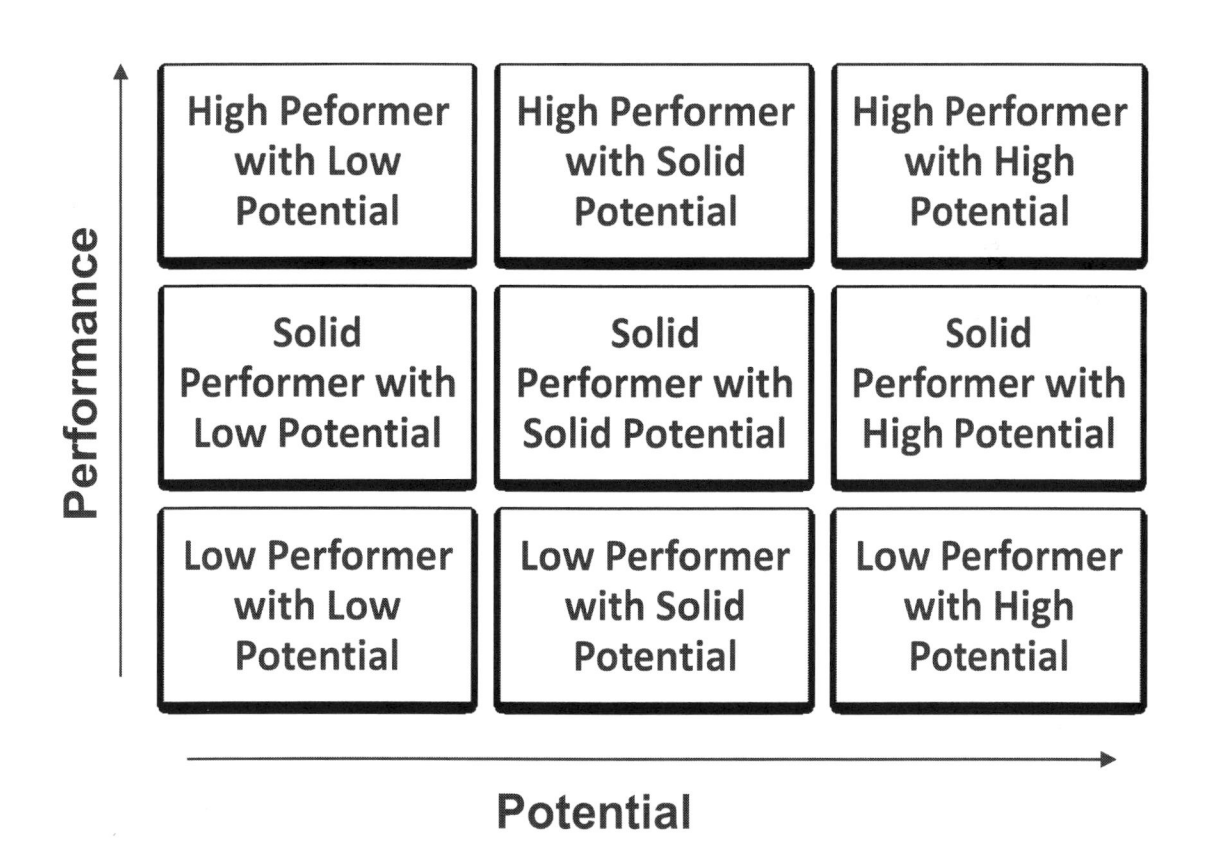

Performance (y-axis) / **Potential** (x-axis)

High Performer with Low Potential	High Performer with Solid Potential	High Performer with High Potential
Solid Performer with Low Potential	Solid Performer with Solid Potential	Solid Performer with High Potential
Low Performer with Low Potential	Low Performer with Solid Potential	Low Performer with High Potential

POSITION COMPETENCY MODELS

Organizations create position competency models for key jobs and/or for job families in the organization. A position competency model provides a map of the ideal knowledge, skills, attributes, abilities, traits, and talents that mirror top performers in that position or job family in the company.

A position competency model will typically include:

- Position qualifications and requirements, such as the education, certifications, knowledge, work experience, etc. that are required to be considered for the position

- A range of attributes that have been proven to lead to success in the position

Once a validated competency model has been created it can be used:

- **To hire new talent**—create job descriptions, position marketing descriptions, hiring assessments, and interview questions.

- **To assess internal talent**—managers can use the competency models to create succession plans and to conduct talent assessments prior to a Talent Review Meeting.

- **To assist employees in career planning**—employees can view the competency models that have been created for careers of interest to them, and they can compare their current competencies and qualifications to the job model. This process enables the employees to identify their strengths, development areas, and qualification gaps for a position and to form a development plan based on this information.

CAREER GROWTH DESCRIPTIONS

As part of the Talent Review process, most organizations use terms and definitions to determine the "career readiness" of each employee reviewed. This action helps the Business Leaders and the HR team to determine the best actions to take over the next year to address career movement and change needs in the organization. The list below shows sample terms and definitions used in the Talent Review process to discuss career readiness:

Typical Terms	Sample Definitions
High Potential, Top Talent, Key Talent	A High Potential demonstrates both the ability <u>AND</u> the desire to advance <u>AND/OR</u> move laterally quickly into 1 or 2 significant new roles over the next few years. A High Potential demonstrates superior business results, excellent people skills, high learning agility, strong leadership potential, and the self-initiative to excel. The total High Potential population is expected to be less than 5% of our total employee population. An employee should have at least 1-year tenure in the company before being nominated for the High Potential program.
Promotable, Ready Now, Advancement Potential	A Promotable employee demonstrates both the ability <u>AND</u> desire to be considered for advancement opportunities. Promotable employees consistently demonstrate strong performance and results; typically Promotable employees will be excellent successors for the next level position. Action should be taken in the coming year to identify a new career growth opportunity in the organization for this employee.
Lateral Placement, Grow Across	Select this option for an employee who could benefit most from a lateral career move into a new functional area to expand knowledge, skills, and job experiences. Lateral moves are encouraged to build a stronger and wider breadth of expertise and to enhance cross-functional knowledge and relationships.
Valued Performer, Solid Performer	A Valued Performer demonstrates dependable performance and an important knowledge and/or skill set that contributes to team and organizational results. The employee is still growing in his/her current position, and the employee can benefit from additional training and new job assignments in this position.
New in Position, Grow in Position, Learner	Select this option for employees who have less than 6 months tenure in their current position and need to remain and grow in this position for at least 12 more months.
Placement Review, Job Fit Adjustment, Performance Issue	If an employee is not currently functioning at least at the Valued Performer level, select this assessment option. The individual may or may not currently be on a performance improvement plan, but improvement is needed, and/or the employee's current position is not a good job fit for the individual. Promotional opportunities are not appropriate for the individual at this time.

IDENTIFYING CRITICAL POSITIONS

In addition to identifying high potentials and successors, organizations may choose to identify critical positions. In this case, we are not looking at people, but we are looking at the impact of the jobs in the organization to determine which positions are most important to focus on for succession planning due to the business impact of the position, and the risk to the organization if the position becomes vacant. This review takes place without factoring in the person who currently holds the position.

Identifying critical positions can be a politically charged process, as everyone certainly wants their own position to be considered critical, and managers certainly want the positions of their own employees to be considered critical. But this practice can assist an organization with a need to focus their talent management budget and time on a small number of positions. The following sample criteria can be used to objectively identify critical positions; the organization can use weighted ratings for the criteria that is most important, and then compare the overall ratings of each position to quickly indentify the most probable critical positions in the organization.

Succession Planning - Critical Position Assessment Tool

Use the scale below to rate each category, to identify the most critical positions to consider for succession planning.

High/Significant = 6
Moderate = 3
Low = 1

© Succession Builders, LLC 2009

Title of Position	Business Impact Level	External Recruiting Difficulty Level	Difficulty Level Finding Internal Successors	Cost of External Recruiting for Position	% of High Vacancy Risk Employees in Position	Succession Plan Focus Rating
Regional Manager	6	3	6	6	1	22
Call Center Director	3	3	6	3	3	18
Financial Strategic Planner	3	3	1	3	6	16
eCommerce Director	6	6	3	6	3	24

In this example, we can see that the eCommerce Director position is the most critical to include in the Talent Review process, because the business impact of the position is high, and it is very difficult and costly to recruit externally for this position.

TALENT ASSESSMENT: RATING LEADERSHIP COMPETENCIES

Another tool you might use as part of your talent assessment process is an evaluation of each individual's strengths and development areas compared to the company's leadership competencies and/or core values. An example of this type of spreadsheet is shown below. **Important:** The behavioral descriptions and rating scale would be provided in a separate Guidebook for Business Leaders to refer to as they are identifying the ratings for each employee.

As the Talent Management Project Lead, you can assist the Business Leaders by analyzing the leadership assessment data prior to the Talent Review Meeting, and by identifying potential questions to ask in the meeting. Review the Leadership Assessment sample below and answer the questions on the following page (NOTE: A rating of "5" is the highest rating, and in this scenario, the leader has referred to behavioral descriptions of each competency on another document to determine the ratings shown below.)

Talent Assessment Data Entry Tool - Steve Sample

Step 1: Assess Past Performance: Leadership Competencies

Competency	Rating
Business Acumen	5
Strategic Thinking	5
Results Orientation	5
People Development	3
Organizational Savvy	1
Decision-Making / Judgment	5
Interpersonal Skills	1
Average: Leadership Competency Ratings	**3.57**

Step 2: Assess Past Performance: Company Values

Value	Rating
Ethics and Integrity	5
Customer Focus	5
Team Builder	3
Accountability	5
Work Ethic	3
Average: Core Competency Ratings	**4.20**

Step 3: Assess Future Potential - Advancement Ability

	Rating
Learning Agility	3
Emotional Intelligence	1
Technical / Functional Skills	5
Advancement Ability	3
Average: Advancement Ability Ratings	**3**

Step 4: Assess Future Potential - Advancement Desire and Engagement

	Rating
Advancement Desire	1
Initiative	5
Intent to Stay	1
Average: Advancement Desire Ratings	**2.33**

Summary of Assessment Results

Past Performance	3.89
Future Potential	2.67
Overall Rating	**3.28**

CASE EXAMPLE: ANALYZING LEADERSHIP ASSESSMENT DATA

An effective Talent Review Meeting Project Lead is able to review talent assessment data and Talent Profile information and identify potential strengths and development needs for the employee under review.

Review **Steve Sample's** Leadership Assessment, and consider your responses to the following questions (Steve is currently a District Manager in the organization):

1. Based on the data, how would you summarize Steve's performance strengths?

2. How would you summarize Steve's development areas?

3. How would you infer these strengths will help him as a leader of other people?

4. What potential struggles might Steve have as a manager, based on this data?

5. What questions would you ask in a Talent Meeting about his future potential?

6. If Steve is being recommended as a Succession Plan successor to an incumbent leader, what questions would you ask the leader?

7. Based on the data, what development actions would you recommend for Steve?

See sample responses to these questions in the Appendix of this Guide.

WHAT SYSTEM WILL YOU USE?

You will need some type of tool or system to gather talent assessment data, and to store talent information.

It is considered to be a best practice to form your policies, practices, and processes first, and then purchase or create your system, rather than having a system form your policies, practices, and processes.

You might use:

- Word documents or Excel Spreadsheets

- Binders of Talent Profiles and Information

- Web-Based Systems

- Your Current Recruiting System, HR System, and/or Learning Management System

Many organizations begin their talent and succession management processes using Word or Excel documents or a simple internally developed online system, while they are forming their own philosophies and procedures. Once the processes are working well in the organization and the volume of data goes beyond what can be handled effectively without an online system, an organization will identify and purchase a Talent Management system, or develop a more robust system internally.

TALENT MANAGEMENT COMMUNICATION IDEAS

Effectively communicating the Talent Management strategy and process to leaders and employees is critical to the success of the initiative each year. The following methods and tools can be used to communicate the Talent Management plans and procedures:

- **A Talent Management Web Site** – Leaders and employees can access the Talent Management System and instructions on this site

- **Talent Management Presentations and/or Webinars** – These virtual training sessions are held each year for leaders to obtain information and updates to the process

- **Management Talking Points** – The Human Resource department can distribute e-mail instructions and "Talking Points" documents to leaders as needed, to guide them through the Talent Management process, to answer employee questions that may arise, and to assist them in the Key Talent notification process

- **Talent Management Guides and/or Quick Reference Guides** – Provides an instructional reference for leaders to reference as they complete each step of the process

> **Your Communication Plan is critical to Talent Management success! Allow at least 6-8 weeks for communication and preparation activities.**

BUSINESS LEADER CONTENT FOR COMMUNICATIONS

As you are creating presentations, training sessions, or reference guides for Business Leaders to document and communicate your Talent Management strategy and processes, use the following foundational list of content to help you get started:

- **What is Talent Management?**

- **Goals of the Organization's Talent Management Strategy**

- **Why Should I Identify Successors?**

- **Define: High Performer, Key Expert, High Potential, Successor**

- **Processes and Tools**

- **Dates and Deadlines**

- **How the Data Will Be Used**

- **Business Leader Action Item Checklist – Next Steps**

SAMPLE: A QUICK REFERENCE TOOL FOR BUSINESS LEADERS

Keep communication tools concise and simple for your busy Business Leaders. One idea is to provide a quick 1-page "Quick Reference Guide" for your leaders, to ensure everyone is clear as to 1) what they need to do, 2) who needs to do it, 3) when does it need to be completed and 4) where do they find the tools required to complete the action?

What Needs to be Done?	Who is Responsible?	What is the deadline?	Where is the tool?
Complete your own Talent Profile—this action creates your internal resume, as well as career interest data pertaining to your own skills, experience and career desires.	All employees in a management position in the organization.	July 15	Click on **People Tools** on the Company Welcome Page and select the **Talent Profile** option. Enter your employee ID to access your form.
Ask your employees in position level 8 or above to complete or update their Talent Profile.	**All** employees in the company are asked to keep their Talent Profile up to date at all times.	July 15	Click on **People Tools** on the Company Welcome Page and select the **Talent Profile** option. Instruct employees to enter their employee ID to access their form.
Schedule and hold a Career and Development meeting with each employee.	**All** leaders in the company are required to hold this meeting with their employees.	August 5	Click on **People Tools** on the Company Welcome Page and select the **Career and Development** option to locate a tool to use for this discussion.
Complete a Talent Assessment—this action provides an opportunity for you to assess and review future leadership talent in your organizational structure, and to nominate employee(s) for the High Potential program.	All employees at level 8 or above in the organization.	August 20	Click on the **Talent Assessment** link on the **Management Tools** web site.
Complete your own Succession Plan – a process of identifying individuals who are Qualified or Future successors to your own position, and the actions needed for development.	All employees at level 8 or above in the organization.	August 20	Click on the **Succession Planning** link on the **Management Tools** web site.

TALKING POINTS FOR LEADERS

Another good communication strategy is to provide "Talking Points" for leaders to help them be prepared for questions from employees, especially if this is the first time you are implementing a Talent Review process in your organization. Examples of Talking Points are shown below:

Q: Can employees apply (or self-nominate) to participate in the High Potential program?

A: No, employees may not self nominate for these programs. High Potentials are selected through the comprehensive process that includes nomination by a direct manager during the online Talent Assessment process, and a structured Talent Review process in which senior leadership teams discuss and agree upon the High Potentials in their business unit. However, employees may self-nominate (with their direct manager's approval) for other professional and leadership development workshops, e-learning courses, and programs in the company.

In addition, leaders are encouraged to discuss that the High Potential development group is not a "static" group, but as a group of employees that will change over time as new candidates will be nominated and reviewed for participation in this program each year. If employees are interested in being considered for this program, they should discuss their performance strengths and development needs with their leaders, be open to feedback, work to leverage their performance strengths, and take action on their development needs.

Q: Will High Potentials be the only ones who are being developed as leaders in the company? Will the company be providing any other leadership development program?

A: As part of our comprehensive Talent Management process, all employees and leaders will be planning and discussing development options that match their specific needs for their current position and for future career plans—employees certainly do not have to be in the High Potential program to be promoted or to obtain training and development.

Q: Will the names of the High Potential employees be announced?

A: No, these names will not be announced publicly; however, the High Potentials themselves will be notified. And like other confidential employee information such as merit increases, incentive pay, and performance review ratings, it is inappropriate for employees to discuss or compare High Potential selections with other employees. And again, it is important to remember that the employees selected to participate in the High Potential program will change on an ongoing basis.

Q: Can I change my successors and nominate new individuals for the High Potential program throughout the year?

A: You can and update your succession plan at any time on the Talent Management system, or by working with your Human Resource Partner. Individuals can only be nominated for the High Potential program once per year, during the formal Talent Assessment and Review process, to ensure a fair, objective, consistent and thorough selection process.

TALKING POINTS FOR LEADERS (CONTINUED)

Q: How should I respond if an employee asks me if they were (or were not) selected for the High Potential program?

A: Prior to the completion of all talent meetings across the entire company, leaders should respond that nominations for the program are still being reviewed and finalized by a team of senior leaders in each business unit. **No employee should be told they were nominated or selected for the High Potential program prior to the calibration and confirmation process that will take place in the Talent Review Meeting.**

Once the names are finalized, leaders will be notified and they will be provided with Talking Points to notify individuals who have been selected for this year's program. Leaders are certainly welcome to discuss the program in general with all employees at any time; however, the names of the individuals selected for the program should not be communicated.

If a leader is asked by an employee why they have not been selected for the program, the leader should meet with the employee to discuss both the employee's strengths and value to the company, as well as development areas that may be preventing the employee from reaching his/her fullest performance potential.

Q: How much should I budget for someone who is selected for the High Potential development program?

A: This year, leaders should budget an average of $5,000 annually for the development of high potentials. The annual Leadership Conference will be budgeted centrally for the High Potential employees in your division.

Q: How much time will a High Potential participant need to spend on his/her development?

A: Each High Potential participant's development plan will vary by individual. However, we expect that each participant will spend at least 80 hours or more in development activities each year.

Q: I would like more information about these leadership development programs and courses available here—how can I obtain this information?

A: Employees can also talk with their Human Resource Partners to obtain more information about our Talent Management strategy and processes, as well as our leadership and professional development programs. Leaders can also find information on our Intranet site on the Human Resources—Leadership Development site pages.

PREPARING THE SENIOR LEADER FOR THE MEETING

Another best practice is to ask the Senior Leader of the group to set the tone for the meeting and to ensure the talent discussions are linked to the business goals of the organization. Key points for the Senior Leader to present to the Talent Review Meeting participants to start the meeting may include:

- The current strategic plan and specific business goals

- The future vision and long-term strategic plan for the organization

- The talent and leadership needs required to achieve this strategy

- Leadership competency needs that will be critical to achieve the strategy

- Specific open and future leadership positions to be filled to achieve the strategy

During the Talent Review Meeting, participants (and the meeting facilitator) should ensure the talent discussions are linked to these business goals. For example, if a key leadership competency to achieve the goals is the ability to see the big picture and to think strategically, the facilitator should ensure the participants discuss the strategic thinking abilities of each individual reviewed in the meeting. If the organization has a critical open leadership position in the area of sales and marketing, the participants and the facilitator will want to listen carefully for individuals with these talents and skills, to identify potential internal candidates for the position.

The Role of the Senior Leader in the Talent Meeting

One of the most important roles of the most senior leader in the Talent Review Meeting is to listen—to listen for:

- New and "up and coming" talent in the organization

- The ability of the leaders in the room to accurately identify, discuss, and develop talent

- The knowledge the leaders in the room have (or potentially don't have) about the people who report to them—their abilities, skills, past work experiences, career interests, etc.

- Critical vacancy risks of key talent in the organization, and to identify retention actions to reduce the risk of losing top talent

TALENT REVIEW MEETING LOGISTICS

The meeting environment can be a surprisingly significant factor in the effectiveness of your Talent Review Meetings. The list below includes some factors to consider if you have influence over the facilities that are selected to hold the Talent Review Meeting:

The size of the room is important:

If the room is too large and participants are spread apart too far from each other, side conversations may start to occur.

In a large room, participants may not be able to hear each other well, and the room size tends to reduce the cohesiveness and energy level of the team discussions, particularly if the participants work in different locations and don't know each other that well in the first place.

If the room is too small, participants feel cramped, irritable, and edgy; this can especially be a problem if the session will be an all day meeting.

Make sure you have the correct audio – visual equipment:

- A projector for viewing employee profiles, presentation slides, etc.

- Internet connectors for meeting participants to check their e-mail during breaks (if desired) and/or for projecting the PPR Online System

- A flip chart for any "parking lot" items that come up that are important for the group but require a different meeting or action to address

Provide adequate refreshments for participants, including coffee, water and soft drinks, and breakfast and lunch if appropriate (if the meeting runs over the lunch period, our recommendation is to ALWAYS provide lunch in the room or the lunch break will run too long).

You may want to provide "fidget items" on the tables if the meeting length will be long, such as foam stress balls, to increase energy and help people focus on the meeting discussion.

NOTE: Talent Review Meetings are most effective when all participants attend the meeting in person. However, if a requirement surfaces for an attendee to participate in the meeting virtually, be sure a conference phone is in the room, make sure the virtual participant has access to all documents and information that will be displayed and used in the meeting.

It is also very important to talk with virtual participants to ensure they will be in a secure location where the meeting discussions <u>will not be heard by anyone else.</u>

SECTION FIVE
FACILITATING THE TALENT REVIEW MEETING

Now that you have completed all of your planning and your talent assessment process, you are ready to schedule and facilitate Talent Review Meeting. This section provides information for the Talent Review Meeting Project Lead to effectively facilitate the meeting.

Remember these key points of facilitation success:

- One of the most important qualities (if not THE most important quality) of a Talent Review Meeting Facilitator is to project confidence and credibility with the leadership team.

- Take time the night before the meeting to review the Talent Profiles and Assessment Data, and make notes regarding points to bring up in the discussion or questions to ask

- It is your job to ask questions and to help the Business Leaders think through their decisions, but remember—this is a business process and ultimately the final decisions made in the Talent Meeting belong to the leaders

- A good rule of thumb to use is that all participants in the Talent Review Meeting must agree that an individual is a successor or a high potential to validate the selection

- Create a chart to track Talent Review Meetings as they are initiated, scheduled, and completed

THE ROLES OF THE TALENT MEETING FACILITATOR

To lead a successful Talent Review Meeting, the facilitator is responsible for these key actions and roles during the meeting:

1. Clarify the agenda and ground rules at the beginning of the meeting.

2. Keep the meeting focused and on track.

3. Know the organization and the talent assessment information and results.

4. Document the meeting – take accurate notes (or ensure the Scribe is taking accurate and concise notes).

5. Ask challenging questions – stimulate rich discussions.

6. Identify and record follow-up and development actions.

STAY OBJECTIVE

Avoid playing a balancing act of facilitator and participant. If you must contribute a data point, make the point in the form of a question, such as, "In this role, the ability to think strategically will be critical. How would you describe Jim's strategic thinking skills?"

FACILITATION TIPS: KEEPING THE MEETING ON TRACK

As the facilitator of the Talent Review Meeting, you have the lead position to keep the meeting on track and on time, and to help ensure that all individuals scheduled to be discussed during the meeting are discussed within the meeting timeline (to avoid rushing through the discussions toward the end of the day). This is actually one of the most challenging roles you have as the Talent Review Meeting Facilitator, because it is easy for participants to take a discussion down a "rabbit trail", to take breaks that are too long, and to "beat a dead horse" by stating the same data point multiple times and in multiple ways. This section provides tips that will help you to be successful in this role.

Tip #1: The first individual discussed in the meeting will take the longest, as the participants are getting used to the format and process of the meeting discussions. Even if you budgeted 15 minutes per individual to be discussed (this is recommended), you will likely find that the first person discussed in the meeting takes at least 30 minutes.

Because you should be using the same process and criteria for each individual to be reviewed, once the leaders have discussed one or two individuals, they should speed up dramatically without being prompted by the facilitator. However, if this doesn't happen "naturally", as the facilitator you will want to point out that the discussions will need to speed up and become more focused and concise, without losing the richness of the discussions.

Tip #2: Use your reflective listening skills frequently to help 1) ensure you understand the behavior and the point of the discussion, and 2) to help bring the discussion to a closure. This is the best technique to use to address the "beating a dead horse syndrome", when you are hearing the same behavior multiple times. For example, "What I hear all of you saying is that David is very detail-oriented, which is a strength for him when completing his reports, but can become a liability when working with clients—is that correct?"

Tip #3: Use the tried-and-true "Parking Lot Flipchart" technique during the Talent Review Meeting to capture "off track" discussions that are important and require off-line discussions and actions. Add the action item to the flipchart to be addressed later on, and then move on with the meeting.

Tip #4: A most effective meeting is one with discussions rather than formal presentations. It is a good idea to very quickly review the Talent Profile of each individual at the beginning of each discussion, to ensure everyone is in sync regarding the individual's qualifications, experience, etc. If time is an issue, it is best for the facilitator to do this, rather than the individual's manager, who will tend to expand on the profile and take much longer, as he or she is proud of having such a talented person on the team (and rightly so). When the facilitator reviews an individual's Talent Profile, it should literally only take about 1 minute, so that the remaining 10-15 minutes for that individual will be spend on rich discussions.

Tip #5: Although you have budgeted 15 minutes to discuss each individual, this is an average amount of time. When you are discussing a new employee and the performance data is very limited, or when discussing a significant performance issue that needs to be addressed after the meeting, spend a smaller amount of time on these individuals as appropriate.

Tip #6: Demonstrate confidence as the Talent Review Meeting Facilitator—don't be afraid to point out to the Business Leaders that the break is over and the meeting needs to start, or that a point has been made and the discussion needs to move forward.

QUESTIONING TECHNIQUES FOR FACILITATORS

As the Talent Review Meeting Facilitator, you are in the position to think objectively about the talent needs, issues, and discussion topics during the Talent Review Meeting. You can increase the effectiveness and results of the Talent Review Meeting by asking questions for clarification, and to bring up an alternative perspective or idea when appropriate. The facilitator should:

Ask questions to obtain additional critical information.

- Example: "What is the impact if this high vacancy risk person leaves?"

Ask questions to pinpoint specific behaviors.

- Example: "What does 'strong technical skills' mean?" (You need to determine if they are talking about computer skills, industry skills, data analysis skills, etc.)

Ask questions to obtain clarification and to take accurate notes.

- Example: "So when you say this individual is 'high maintenance', are you saying they need to develop stress management skills, or corporate maturity when handling change…"

Ask questions to determine the impact of a leader's behavior.

- Example: "So when you say this leader is lacking coaching skills, is this affecting the team's turnover, development, ability to handle performance issues…?"

Ask questions to help participants see another perspective or the "bigger picture".

- Example: "You are identifying this leader as an executive-level high potential; they currently have 2 years of leadership experience…will they be ready for an executive role?"

Ask questions to identify how a leader's strength can be better leveraged.

- Example: "You said this leader is excellent at spotting talent and interviewing effectively – how can you leverage this strength on your team?"

Ask questions to find out the "why" behind the statements.

- Example: "Why do you think this person is at low risk of leaving?"

Ask questions to find out what actions have already been taken to develop the individual, and to learn more about the individual's career interests and development goals.

- Example: "When you coached this person on their communication style, how have they accepted and applied the feedback on the job?"

SAMPLE TALENT REVIEW DISCUSSION

While it is difficult to provide any type of "generic" Talent Review Meeting discussion because each organization will have a different strategy and approach, this section attempts to provide a sample conversation that might take place in a Talent Review Meeting.

The discussion depicted below would take place following all of the beginning phases of the meeting, such as reviewing the meeting agenda and ground rules, introduction of each meeting participant, and the senior leader presentation of the business goals and talent needs to focus on during the Talent Review Meeting.

Facilitator: The first manager we will review is Lee Howard. (Facilitator projects Lee's Talent Profile on a viewing screen for the participants to view.)

We can see from Lee's profile that he has been with the company for 6 years, and he has been in his current Financial Manager position for 2 years. Previously, Lee was with the BANK Corporation as an Accounting Analyst for 5 years. Lee has a Bachelor's degree in Accounting, he is a CPA. His most recent performance review rating was Outstanding. Lee is open to relocation. Would anyone like to add anything else to this information about Lee's Talent Profile?

Lee's Manager: Lee just completed his MBA but it just hasn't been added to his Talent Profile yet.

Facilitator: Great – we can add that to his profile. Let's first discuss Lee's Vacancy Risk – would you say that there is a High, Moderate, or Low chance that Lee will leave the organization within the next 12 months?

Lee's Manager: I think there is a Moderate chance that Lee will leave the organization.

Facilitator: Okay—why do you think this is the case?

Lee's Manager: Well, last year I said that there was only a Low chance that Lee would leave, because he has always been happy here and he enjoys his work. But he has been talking about wanting more challenge and more career opportunity, and especially now that he just completed his MBA, I think that we could lose him if we don't start looking at some career movement or advancement opportunities for him.

The HR Partner (for Lee's Division): I agree; Lee came to talk with me about career opportunities just a few weeks ago.

Facilitator: What would be the business impact if Lee does leave?

Lee's Manager: Well, we do have other Financial Managers who could take on some of Lee's responsibilities if he were to leave, although it would put a pretty heavy burden on them. The biggest loss to the company is that I think Lee has a lot of potential for the Director level in the Financial Division, and possibly even potential for a Vice President level leadership role.

Facilitator: So it sounds like we have a strong business case for taking action to retain Lee. And it sounds like career opportunities are the most important issue to Lee if we want to retain him—is that correct?

Lee's Manager: Yes, that is correct, and I am also sure that he is interested in more compensation as well, as I know he invested a lot into his own MBA program.

HR Partner: Yes, Lee discussed that as well when we talked. He is interested in both advancement opportunities and ways to enhance both is responsibility level and his compensation.

Facilitator: Okay, let's go ahead and discuss Lee's strengths and development needs, and then talk about potential career growth ideas for him. What would you say are key strengths for Lee?

Lee's Manager: Lee's financial knowledge is outstanding, and he knows our own financial strategy and processes inside and out. He has a strong network in the company, and he works well with pretty much everyone. He is very well respected.

Other Financial Manager: I worked with Lee on the budgeting project. He was always prepared for the meetings, and is very detail-oriented.

Lee's Manager: Yes, sometimes he can be too detail-oriented.

Facilitator: Okay, it sounds like being detail-oriented is both a strength and sometimes a liability for Lee. Let's go ahead and continue with his strengths and then we'll go on to his development areas. What other strengths do you see for Lee?

HR Partner: All of Lee's team respect him and I don't have any management issues in his group. He does a good job of meeting with his direct reports, providing feedback, getting his performance reviews done on time, and handling performance issues. I see him as a strong people leader.

Lee's Manager: I agree—he works well with others in the company and he treats his own employees with the same respect. He also has strong technical skills.

Facilitator: When you say Lee has strong technical skills, are you referring to computer technical skills, or financial process skills, or…?

Lee's Manager: I meant that Lee is really good with the computer. Ask him to set up a complicated Excel worksheet, and he is in heaven.

Facilitator: Okay—any other strengths that we should document for Lee?

Other Financial Manager: He's kind of a "go-to" guy—people seek him out when they need some help analyzing data or figuring out a computer problem.

Facilitator: Okay, thank you—let's now go on to Lee's development areas. We've already noted that sometimes his detail-orientation can be a liability for Lee. Can someone expand on this?

Lee's Manager: When Lee is working with Business Leaders regarding budget or reporting issues, he often discusses so much detail level that the manager starts to tune him out or simply doesn't understand what he is talking about. Also, sometimes Lee will miss a deadline because he keeps analyzing data over and over to make sure he hasn't missed anything. It is great that I know he is so careful to make sure his numbers are correct, but sometimes he needs more of a balance to know when to see the bigger picture.

Other Financial Manager: Yes, sometimes when we are in meetings together, Lee is so analytical and so detailed that others get frustrated with him.

Facilitator: When you've given feedback to Lee about this, what has his response been?

Lee's Manager: I haven't really talked with Lee about this issue.

Facilitator: Okay, how about if we put as an action item to provide some feedback to Lee about this issue. Also, what if we did a 360 feedback process to include the Business Leaders he works with so he can see his strengths and development needs from the perspective of his internal customers?

Lee's Manager: Okay, those are both good ideas.

Facilitator: What other development areas should we note for Lee?

Lee's Manager: Really that is the main one. He also needs to increase his ability to give a presentation to senior leaders—to be more concise in his presentations.

Facilitator: I know of a workshop that addresses the skill area of advanced presentation skills, including the skills of modifying a presentation to meet the audience needs, and presenting to executive level leaders. I could put this on the list of action items for Lee, and I can send an e-mail to you with information and the workshop web site link. Would that help Lee to address this development area?

Lee's Manager: Yes, it would be fine to make a note on that and to send the information to me.

Facilitator: Are there any other development areas to be discussed for Lee, or are we ready to move on?

Lee's Manager: We can move on.

Facilitator: Let's discuss Lee's career movement potential. Earlier we discussed the Lee has expressed an interest in some career growth and a new opportunity, so we know he has the desire for this. Does the group also see that Lee has the ability for career growth at this time?

Lee's Manager: Yes, I think that Lee has already learned everything there is to know in his current position, and as I said before, I think we might lose him if we don't find something for him here that is more challenging.

HR Manager (Maria): I agree completely.

Other Financial Manager (Ann): Yes, I also agree, and I have a new position that is pending budget approval at the director level—I think if that position is approved it would be a potential opportunity for Lee.

Facilitator: Okay, so short term—within the next year—it sounds like everyone agrees that Lee is ready for career growth and/or advancement, so I'll make a note of that. And we have one possibility for Lee for a director-level position in Ann's department. Now that position is currently located in Chicago and Lee is in St. Louis. So first of all, would Lee be able to function in this position in Ann's department from St. Louis, or would he need to relocate? Secondly, would Lee be willing to relocate for this position?

Ann: Yes, he would need to relocate in order to effectively manage a large team reporting to him.

Lee's Manager (Pierre): Yes, when he and I discussed his career interests, he said he was completely open to relocating for the right position.

Facilitator: Okay—when will we know if this position has been funded?

Ann: I will know next month, and I will let Pierre and Maria know if it is funded so we can then talk with Lee about the position.

Facilitator: That sounds like a good plan and I'll make a note of this in the action plan area. Are there any other positions that might be a good fit for Lee that would be a growth opportunity for him?

Maria: If he is willing to move into an Operations role and take a challenging lateral position, we have an Operations Manager position open in the St. Louis site right now.

Lee's Manager: I think with his attention to detail and ability to execute processes this type of role might be a good fit for him. I can go ahead and start talking with him about that now to see what his interest level is, and then I'll have him get in touch with you if he is interested in the position.

Facilitator: Great—I'll make a note of this in the action plans. Where do we see Lee moving in the next 2-3 years?

Lee's Manager: I think we need to see how he does in one of these new roles before we can determine that. However, I do think if he does well he has Vice President career potential.

Facilitator: Okay, let's recap our action plans for Lee and then we'll need to move on to the next individual. Pierre (Lee's Manager) is going to provide some feedback to Lee about how to continue to leverage his detail orientation strength while addressing the issues that occur when he becomes too detailed. I will send information to Pierre about the Executive Presentation Skills Workshop. Ann will let Pierre and Maria know when she receives word that the new Director position in her department is funded. Pierre will also talk with Lee about the Operations Manager position that is currently open to see if he would like to interview for this position.

Is there anything else anyone would like to add to our notes and action plans for Lee? Okay, let's move on to discuss Ben Murdock…

DOCUMENTING THE MEETING – SCRIBE RESPONSIBILITIES

As the Talent Review Meeting Facilitator, you will be leading the participants through the discussion process. But the role of the Scribe is equally important—if the discussions are not captured in an accurate and readable manner, some of the value that the meeting provides will be lost. In addition, it is important to know that if any legal situations occur with an employee discussed in a Talent Review meeting, the notes taken in the meeting could be considered discoverable data, and so it is very important to ensure the notes are accurate and written in a legal and appropriate manner.

Here are some tips to effectively scribe the Talent Review Meeting:

- Don't ask an Administrative Assistant at the last minute to take notes in the meeting. Normally when an Assistant takes notes in a meeting, their role is to write extensive and very detailed notes, and what you want in this situation is a concise record of high level points and action plans. If you do want to ask an Assistant to serve as a scribe in the meeting, provide some training and direction prior to the meeting.

- The scribe should be prepared for keeping up with the "speed" of the meeting conversations to help ensure the discussions are able to flow freely without waiting for the scribe on a frequent basis. However, the Scribe does have a right to ask the participants to repeat a key point, to ask questions for clarity, and to ask participants to speak up if needed.

- The facilitator can assist the scribe by repeating a key point, or rephrasing what the participants said in a concise way, which helps the scribe to document the point in a concise way, as well as checking to ensure the facilitator (and the meeting participants) accurately understands the point. Use a reflective listening technique to achieve this, such as, "So it sounds like you are saying that if we don't provide a more challenging role to Hannah soon, her vacancy risk will be high, is that correct?"

- It is not recommended to tape the meeting in any way. First of all, this might reduce the open communication in the meeting. Also, sometimes, despite your best efforts to review the Ground Rules, meeting participants will say something that frankly you don't want to be recorded. In addition, if you record the discussions, you will still need someone to review the video or audio recording and create more concise, actionable notes. And there is always the risk that the recording technology doesn't work, resulting in lost notes.

- It works very well to project the notes on a screen that the scribe is writing during the meeting, so the participants can:

    o See that their points are being documented accurately

    o Make corrections "real-time" as needed in the notes

    o Continue to read all of the notes during the discussion to form an overall picture of the individual's strengths, development needs and action plans

SCRIBE NOTES EXAMPLE

The chart below shows an example of the type of notes a Scribe in the Talent Review Meeting might write.

Name of Individual Reviewed: Lee Ming, Financial Manager

Time in Company	6 years
Time in Position	2 years
Vacancy Risk	Moderate: Just completed MBA—has expressed interest in advancement and challenging career growth opportunities.
Vacancy Business Impact	Moderate: Responsibilities could be covered by others until the position is filled again. However, the company would lose a strong leader with Director / VP potential.
Strengths	Excellent financial acumen knowledge and credentials—Accounting Degree, CPA, MBA. Well respected—a "go-to person" in the organization, and well networked. Attention to detail is strong. Strong interpersonal skills and leadership skills. Follows through well and executes processes well.
Development Areas	Sometimes Lee's attention to detail can become a problem for internal customers who just need a concise explanation, and when Lee is presenting to executives. Lee needs to obtain a better balance to know when to complete an analysis in order to make a decision or to meet a deadline on time.
Short-Term Career Potential	Lee has potential within the next year for a Director level position. Alternatively, Lee could take on a challenging lateral move at the Manager level.
Long-Term Career Potential	Lee has potential in the next few years for a VP level position, depending on his performance at the next level.
Action Plans	Pierre will coach Lee about balancing his attention to detail and to be more concise when needed. Sam will send information to Pierre about the Executive Presentation Skills Workshop. Ann will meet with Pierre and Maria when she receives notification that the new Director position in her department is funded. Pierre will also talk with Lee about the Operations Manager position to determine his interest in this career path.

SECTION SIX
AFTER THE TALENT REVIEW MEETING

This section provides information for the Talent Review Meeting Project Lead to make effective use of the talent data, to make development recommendations and to measure results. In this section we will also discuss the issue of High Potential notification.

To increase the follow through and completion of Talent Management actions and Talent Review Meeting development plans, the following ideas and procedures can serve to reward people development actions and to enhance accountability for leadership development:

- **Leaders are measured on their talent management and employee development results on their annual performance appraisal**

- **Leaders prepare a Talent Management Summary report or presentation to provide to their leader (or to the Board of Directors, as applicable for the leadership level); a percentage of each leader's annual merit bonus is tied to the completion of these succession planning activities**

- **Each Talent Review Meeting held increases accountability (leaders will want to show they have followed through with their action items in front of their peers)**

- **Employees identified for participation in the Key Talent program will have an annual "3-way meeting" with their manager and an HR Partner, to review:**

    o The development actions completed

    o What the Key Talent employee has learned from the development actions completed

    o How the Key Talent employee applied new learning to their job function

SAMPLE QUESTIONS – POST TALENT REVIEW EVALUATION

After the Talent Review Meetings, obtain feedback from the Business Leader participants regarding the meeting effectiveness and the value of the Talent Review session (just as we typically will do following a training workshop to obtain customer satisfaction and ideas for continuous improvement). This feedback can be obtained in interviews with Business Leaders, and/or in a survey format.

Sample questions to include on this type of Post Talent Review Meeting feedback or interview survey are shown below.

NOTE: Be sure to also gather some demographic information on the survey, such as the management level of the respondent, and how many times the respondent has attended a Talent Review Meeting previously. As one example, you may want to analyze this data to determine if leaders who have previously attended a Talent Review Meeting feel more prepared for the meeting than first-time attendees.

1. Prior to the Talent Review Meeting, did you receive all of the information you needed to be fully prepared for the meeting? What tools and information were most helpful as you prepared for the meeting? What suggestions do you have to help improve our communication and preparation process prior to the Talent Review Meeting?

2. As you prepared for the Talent Review Meeting, did you contact your Human Resource Partner or Talent Management Director? If so, was this individual able to assist you?

3. During the meeting, did the Talent Review facilitator lead the meeting effectively by providing a good balance of structure and format while also facilitating rich discussions?

4. At the beginning of the Talent Review Meeting, were the business goals and talent needs for your organization clearly discussed to provide the focus and direction of the meeting?

5. Was the agenda of the meeting provided to you prior to the meeting? Did the facilitator review meeting guidelines at the beginning of the session?

6. Did the Talent Review Meeting Facilitator keep the meeting on track and on time?

7. Did the Talent Review Meeting facilitator or a separate scribe take accurate notes during the meeting?

8. Was the Talent Review Meeting facilitator fully prepared for the meeting?

9. Did the meeting enhance your knowledge of the talented employees, emerging leaders, and current leaders in the organization?

10. Did this meeting serve to strengthen the relationships of the leaders in your organization? Why or why not?

11. Was the Talent Review Meeting a valuable use of your time? Why or why not?

12. What is your trust level that the information discussed in the Talent Review Meeting will be used appropriately and effectively to enhance performance and business results?

TALENT REVIEW MEETING FACILITATOR FEEDBACK FORM

Use the form below to provide feedback and coaching to a new Talent Review Meeting Facilitator:

Succession Builders.com	Talent Review Meeting Facilitator Certification Feedback Form for _____ Coaching Meeting Held on _____

Did the Talent Review Meeting Facilitator follow a consistent agenda and format throughout the meeting?
Was the facilitator prepared for the meeting – did the facilitator clearly study talent assessments and profiles?
Did the facilitator keep the meeting on track and on time?
Did the facilitator achieve the goals and the agenda objectives of the meeting?
Did the facilitator work as a partner with the meeting scribe to ensure accurate notes were taken in the meeting?
Did the facilitator use reflective listening techniques to ensure accuracy and to help participants conclude a point?
If any conflict or opposing views occurred in the meeting, how did the facilitator handle this?
Did the facilitator demonstrate and project confidence and leadership during the meeting?
As a scribe, did the facilitator accurately record notes from the discussions?
As a scribe, did the facilitator keep notes concise but detailed enough to avoid any confusion at a later point?
What are key strengths of this facilitator?
What are key development areas for this facilitator?
Document development actions here:

HIGH POTENTIAL NOTIFICATION: YOU HAVE CHOICES!

The notification of High Potentials and/or Key Experts continues to be a very controversial topic in the Human Resources function. A clear best practice has not yet emerged. However, it is important to understand that "to tell or not to tell" is not a clear-cut decision – you have choices:

- **You can notify all employees of their talent standing**
- **You can notify High Potentials only**
- **You can notify the managers of the High Potentials**
- **You can notify only specific Human Resource or Business Leaders in the company**

> **A high potential notification choice that is not recommended is to leave the notification decision up to each manager, or to not have a notification policy. Because employees talk with each other across management groups, this could cause many potential problems, such as a perception that the process is unfair, or that some managers in the company are developing their employees but others are not.**

Companies can use the following chart to help make this decision—consider the goals of your talent strategy and the culture of your organization when determining your notification plan:

Advantages of Notifying	Advantages of Not Notifying
Results in a higher retention rate of High Potentials	Reduces concern regarding morale issues of employees not currently identified as High Potentials
Increases the ability to provide development resources and programs to High Potentials	Promotes an environment that all employees are expected to be high performers
Increases the ability to measure the results of the High Potential Program	Reduces concern about the need to move employees out of the High Potential program in the future
Results in a greater transparency pertaining to career development to motivate employees	Eliminates the cost and time required to provide focused development opportunities for High Potentials
Increases the ability to create and execute cross-functional career moves for High Potentials	Emphasizes the development strategy that each manager is responsible for providing on-the-job development

A SAMPLE TALENT NOTIFICATION PROCESS

During the Talent Review Meetings, employees may be identified for your High Potential development program. At the appropriate time after the Talent Review Meetings are all completed, employees who have been identified for this program can be notified, using the following process:

Step 1: Leaders will receive information and talking points from HR when it is time to notify Key Talent employees. Leaders will review the Talent Management system to determine which direct reports have been selected for the program.

Step 2: Leaders notify their Key Talent employees, and direct them to send an e-mail to HR to obtain their "Next Steps" information.

Step 3: Key Talent employees will be notified by HR to attend a "Kickoff Session" to begin their development program. This session will provide information about the Key Talent program and development resources.

WHAT DO THEY NEED TO KNOW?

Using appropriate talent management data security practices is a critical role for the Talent Management Professional. It is important to maintain the correct balance between providing talent data to drive cross-functional career movement and development, while also ensuring the appropriate confidentiality level to protect the information.

Record your policy regarding the talent and succession plan data security level for each of the following groups, and the methods and/or tools that provide the data to this group. For example, will your C-level executives all have access to the entire list of high potential employees and successors? How about senior level leaders – will they also have access to this same information for the entire company, or will they only have this information for their own divisions? Will everyone in the Recruiting function have access to all succession plan information, or will only senior or management level Recruiting professionals have access to this information?

Employee Group	What Talent Information Will They Receive?
Executives	
Senior Leaders	
Mid-Level Leaders	
Learning and Development	
Human Resource Partners	
Recruiting Function	
Other?	

HOW DO I DEVELOP HIGH POTENTIAL EMPLOYEES?

Provide a combination of on-the-job development opportunities, new job assignments and formal development workshops and resources to your high potential employees. As much as possible, create "two-way" development actions that provide business results for the organization and development results for the high potential employee.

Examples of these "two-way" development actions include:

Development Action	The High Potential will build…	The organization…
High Potentials serve on critical project teams.	…leadership skills, strategic thinking, cross-functional relationships and project management skills.	…benefits from having top talent contribute ideas and strategic thinking to the most critical issues.
High Potentials move laterally and cross-functionally into new positions, in addition to taking on advancement career opportunities over time.	…a wider breadth of knowledge, skills and experience, and wider network across the company.	…benefits by developing leaders with an enhanced understanding of the goals and issues faced by the different departments, functions and regions of the company.
High Potentials serve in mentor and/or training roles to others in the company.	…the ability to develop others, to present information effectively, and to coach others.	…benefits from the training and information provided by a top resource from within the company, rather than always paying for external training resources.

LEADERSHIP DEVELOPMENT IDEAS—BE CREATIVE!

Each employee should have a development plan that is discussed and updated during the year. Consider a variety of development options and remember that employees learn the most from on-the-job assignments, such as taking on a new job responsibility, serving on a new project team, or resolving a challenging issue.

While some excellent development resources do require a budget, many of the best development ideas cost little or nothing other than an investment of time. A leadership and high potential development program should include multiple development options.

To obtain new knowledge, skills, and leadership experience, high potential leaders can:

Serve on a Project Team	Obtain 360 Feedback and Coaching
Participate in Leadership Workshops	Participate in a Leadership Book Club
Obtain an Executive Mentor or Sponsor	Present at an Industry Conference
Serve on a Non-Profit Board	Serve as a Community Service Leader
Obtain a Job Rotation Assignment	Publish in an Industry Periodical
Complete an E-Learning Course	Mentor New Employees
Develop Internal Procedure Guides	Develop / Deliver Internal Training
Complete a New Degree or MBA	Attend Industry Association Meetings
Participate in a Business Simulation	Take on a New Job Stretch Assignment
Join a Local Toastmasters Group	Participate in a Research Project
Obtain / Update a Certification	Work with an Executive Coach

CASE EXAMPLE: MAKING DEVELOPMENT RECOMMENDATIONS

Using the Talent Review Meeting notes, what action plans and development recommendations would you suggest for each of these leaders? Remember to consider a wide variety of development resources, focusing primarily on "on-the-job" development actions. Record your ideas on the following page.

Name and Title	Vacancy Risk and Impact	Next Likely Move	Strengths	Development Areas
Lee Ling, Vice President	Low, Low	Just started in the Vice President role.	Strong interpersonal communication skills. Good at project management and analyzing data. Strong work ethic – dedicated to the company. Respected at all levels in the organization. Very responsive to customers.	Needs more visibility with senior management. Needs to increase appropriate assertiveness and demonstrate more confidence in meetings.
Mahar Patel, Manager	High, Low	Needs to perform current job at a higher level first.	Strong computer skills, especially Excel spreadsheets. Strong industry background and knowledge.	Not a teamplayer—does not collaborate effectively on projects. Needs to increase ability to coach employees and address performance issues. Does not always follow through or meet deadlines. Turnover in Mahar's staff is more than 60%.
Luis LaPorte, Director	Low, Moderate	Could move into an HR or Finance role, as a lateral move.	Dependable. Identifies process improvements and executes change effectively. Detail oriented – follows through on details well. Good at solving problems.	Needs to increase his ability to think strategically. Needs to enhance presentation skills and to influence others. Needs to increase knowledge of our industry.
Jane Gordon, Director	Low, Low	Jane's current position is a good fit for the next year. Her responsibilities were just expanded.	Demonstrates a consistently positive communication style. Strong interpersonal skills – works well with everyone. Demonstrates strong corporate maturity and handles stress and ambiguous situations very well. Stays calm in a crisis.	Needs to learn project management and time management skills. Has a tendency to miss details.
Michelle Mao, Director	High, High	Is ready for a promotion to the next level this year. Might also be effective in the Sales group.	Negotiates well. Demonstrates strong team building skills. Is a great presenter – demonstrates strong speaking and written communication skills. Gets the job done and follows through with details, but also looks at issues from a strategic standpoint. Strong financial acumen.	Needs to learn more about the company. Needs to increase her visibility in the organization and to broaden her internal network outside of the organization.

CASE EXAMPLE: DEVELOPMENT RECOMMENDATION NOTES

What action plans and development recommendations would you make for Lee Ling?

What action plans and development recommendations would you make for Mahar Patel?

What action plans and development recommendations would you make for Luis LaPorte?

What action plans and development recommendations would you make for Jane Gordon?

What action plans and development recommendations would you make for Michelle Mao?

See sample responses to this exercise in the Appendix of this book.

TALENT MANAGEMENT METRICS

The metrics used to measure the effectiveness and return-on-investment of the Talent Management strategy provides information to the company and to our Business Leaders about the overall status and strength of their leadership teams, and for the leadership strengths and risks for the entire organization.

The metrics fall into the following categories:

- **General Leadership Population Metrics**, such as the ratio of leaders to employees, diversity statistics of the leadership population, etc.

- **Leadership Development Metrics**, such as the percentage of leaders with a Development Plan, tracking completion of leadership training requirements, etc.

- **Leadership Benchstrength and Succession Plan Metrics**, such as the percentage of leaders who have at least one Prepared Successor, the Vacancy Risk percentages of leaders by department, the percentage of successors who eventually fill the position they are identified for, etc.

- **High Potential Population Metrics**, such as the percentage of individuals in the company identified as a High Potential, the diversity statistics of the High Potential population, etc.

- **Talent Review Meeting Metrics**, such as evaluation ratings from the surveys leaders complete following a Talent Review meeting (see page 88 for sample evaluation survey questions)

- **Return-On-Investment Metrics**, such as the percentage of time a leadership position is filled internally versus the cost of external fill of leadership positions, retention of high potential employees, etc.

- **Location or Global Leadership Movement Metrics**, such as job rotational metrics, global job assignment statistics, changes in leadership populations by country, etc.

COMMUNICATE YOUR RESULTS

Just as it is important to communicate your Talent Management strategy effectively during the planning and preparation process, it is just as important to communicate discoveries that resulted from the Talent Review Meetings and to communicate business results from the process.

You may want to create reports and/or presentations to communicate your findings. Some examples of data to communicate include:

- Overall Talent Review Meeting Participation and Feedback
- Graphed high-level results of vacancy risk, succession plan data, etc.
- Themes and trends that emerged from the talent discussions
- Development recommendations
- Action plans and "Next Steps"

Use charts and graphs to display your results in a concise manner whenever possible; examples of these types of charts are shown below:

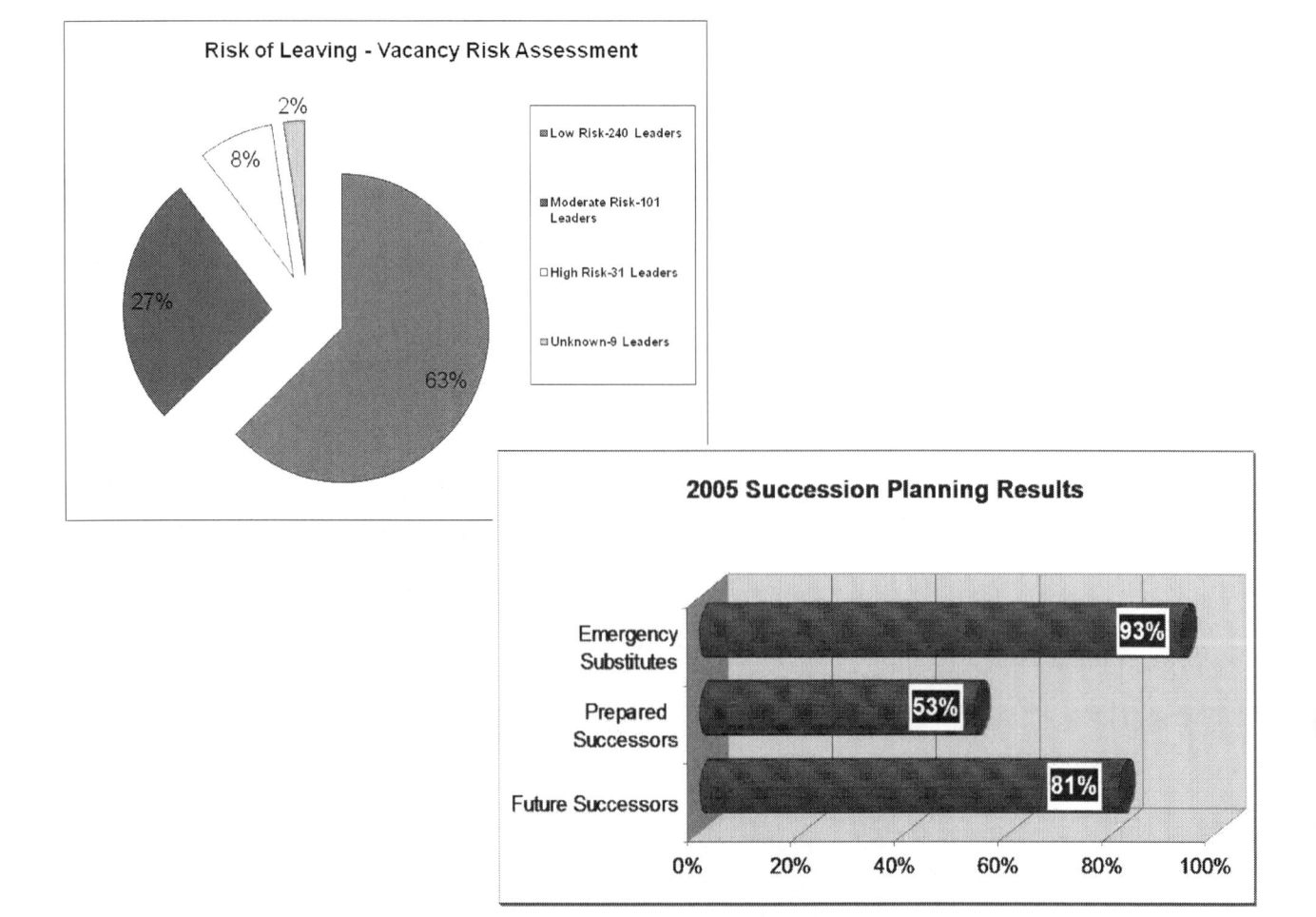

APPENDIX

This section contains answers to fill-in-the-blank and case example exercises in this book for your reference.

In addition, in this section you will find answers to frequently-asked questions about talent management, succession planning, and high potential identification and development.

TALENT MANAGEMENT CONCEPTS: SAME AND DIFFERENT

Talent Management ⟷ Performance Management		
How are they similar? Both are designed to review and enhance employee performance.		
✓ Looks at FUTURE potential ✓ Typically measures multiple dimensions pertaining to performance and potential ✓ Focuses more on longer term business needs and the "bigger picture" organizational performance		✓ Looks at PAST performance ✓ Typically measures 2 dimensions: goals and behaviors ✓ Typically has a short-term focus, providing feedback to individual employees regarding the achievement of last year's business goals

Successors ⟷ High Potentials		
How are they similar? Both are designed to improve the company's leadership pipeline.		
✓ Identified as an individual who could move into one or more specific positions ✓ A successor may be a high performer or a high potential employee ✓ Organizations should have many more successors than high potential employees		✓ Identified as an individual who could move up and across into <u>multiple</u> positions and departments ✓ Typically a high potential population size is less than 10% of the employee population

High Performers ⟷ High Potentials		
How are they similar? Both are critical to the success of the organization.		
✓ Demonstrates a strong work ethic, achieves results, demonstrates effective interpersonal skills, etc. ✓ May not have the desire or the ability to move cross-functionally in their career, or to advance into multiple leadership positions		✓ A subset of the total high performing population of employees ✓ A high potential is a high performer who ALSO desires leadership advancement, shows high initiative and superior learning agility, is highly engaged, and has the potential for advancement and challenging career roles.

CASE EXAMPLE: PLANNING A TALENT REVIEW MEETING

Answer the following questions, and form an agenda and timing for the meeting below:

1. How many Talent Review Meetings will be needed for this group?

   Three meetings are recommended:

   1) A 1-on-1 meeting with the EVP to review his/her succession plan and the SVP leaders
   2) A meeting with the three SVPs to review their succession plans and their VP team
   3) A full-length meeting with the VPs to review their succession plans and the 20 leaders

2. How will you handle the participant who wants to participate in the meeting virtually?

It is not recommended for this person to attend virtually. First, it is the guideline (and best practice) for leaders to attend Talent Review Meetings in person. Secondly, the leader requesting the virtual participation has never seen or participated in a talent meeting, and therefore has no previous experience (or probably skill level) in this area.

3. What might be some special considerations for this group that could affect the timing or effectiveness of the meeting, and what action(s) could you take as the facilitator to address these issues?

Check with the HR manager of the group to determine their "group style", but typically a sales group wants to keep things moving pretty quickly, so you'll need to balance their desire for a brief meeting with the need to execute an effective talent meeting for this group.

Also, a sales group typically has a short attention span as they are always thinking about their pending sales and the deals they have going on. It might work better to have two half-day sessions rather than a full 1-day session – explore scheduling options with them.

4. Enter the Agenda and timing for a Talent Review Meeting to meet this group's needs:

Timing	Agenda Item - Description
30 Minutes	Participants Gathering, Introductions, Agenda, Ground Rules
30 Minutes	Senior Leader presentation of the group's business goals, the talent needs to achieve the goals, and any current and future leadership positions
3.5 Hours	Review the vacancy risks, strengths, development needs, career potential of 12 leaders (10 minutes each leader X 20 leaders = approximately 3.5 hours;) NOTE: For the sales team that wants to move quickly and talks quickly, the facilitator can use the 10 minute per person guideline. In addition, almost all of the participants have been through a Talent Review meeting before, which will speed up the discussion.
1 Hour	Reviewing nominated high potentials or top talent
1 Hour	Discuss the VP level Replacement Planning charts
1 Hour	Breaks and Lunch throughout the day
7.5 Hours	**Total Meeting time**

CASE EXAMPLE: ANALYZING LEADERSHIP ASSESSMENT DATA

An effective Talent Review Meeting Project Lead is able to review talent assessment data and Talent Profile information and identify potential strengths and development needs for the employee under review.

Review **Steve Sample's** Leadership Assessment, and consider your responses to the following questions (Steve is currently a District Manager in the organization):

1. **Based on the data, how would you summarize Steve's performance strengths?**
   Steve is a highly results-oriented individual who demonstrates strong knowledge and expertise. He is very customer focused and has a strong work ethic. He always "gets the job done".

2. **How would you summarize Steve's development areas?**
   All of Steve's development areas pertain to his people skills. He does not currently demonstrate strong interpersonal skills.

3. **How would you infer these strengths help him as a leader of other people?**
   Steve's strengths will lend credibility as a leader to his team. He will likely be good at holding others accountable for results, because he holds himself accountable. His team can learn from his expertise and knowledge.

4. **What potential struggles might Steve have as a manager, based on this data?**
   Steve will probably have to learn how to let go of his own role of expertise and develop the employees on his team. He will need to develop his interpersonal skills in order to effectively coach his team and to communicate with his management peers.

5. **What questions would you ask in a Talent Meeting about his future potential?**
   Is Steve open to developing his interpersonal and leadership skills? Does Steve want to be a leader? Is he interested in advancement? What can you tell me about his vacancy risk?

6. **If Steve is being recommended as a Succession Chart successor to an incumbent leader, what questions would you ask the leader?**
   Is he willing to relocate? Does Steve want to be a leader? Is Steve interested in this position?

7. **Based on the data, what development actions would you recommend for Steve?**
   A good formal development option for Steve is to attend foundational leadership workshops pertaining to coaching, delegation and transitioning into the leadership role. Steve would also benefit by having an experienced manager serve as a mentor to him, especially a mentor who has superior people skills.

CASE EXAMPLE: DEVELOPMENT RECOMMENDATION NOTES

What action plans and development recommendations would you make for Lee Ling?

Because Lee just started in a Vice President role, what he needs most is a mentor or an executive coach to transition effectively into this new role. An internal mentor could also help him make connections in the company with other leaders to increase his visibility.

What action plans and development recommendations would you make for Mahar Patel?

Given Mahar's high vacancy risk, low business impact and significant performance issues, the facilitator should determine what performance improvement actions have already been taken to improve the situation. It may be appropriate to suggest a formal performance improvement plan for Mahar.

What action plans and development recommendations would you make for Luis LaPorte?

Luis should receive coaching to ensure he understands his development needs; a formal Strategic Thinking workshop may be helpful. A lateral move into a position that requires a more strategic role may be helpful, if Luis is interested in advancement and career growth. If not, Luis may be considered a solid performer in his current role, and continue to receive development and coaching to meet his needs, as well as opportunities to work on assignments that leverage his detail-oriented strength.

What action plans and development recommendations would you make for Jane Gordon?

Jane is doing very well in her current role, and she simply needs to develop more self-management skills. A time management and project management workshop and ongoing feedback from her manager in these areas should address these needs.

What action plans and development recommendations would you make for Michelle Mao?

Michelle demonstrates the characteristics of a high employee, based on the extensive list of strengths. She is ready for a promotional opportunity, and action should be taken to identify potential opportunities for her and to discuss her career interests. A higher-level sponsor would help her increase her internal network and visibility.

FREQUENTLY ASKED QUESTIONS

This section is a summary of frequently asked questions and answers concerning talent management.

Question: Should we audio-record a Talent Review Meeting?

Answer: Audio-recording a Talent Review Meeting is not recommend for the following reasons:

- It is always important to remember that Talent Review Meeting data could be used for legal purposes, such as an audit or court discovery process, and occasionally some of the verbally spoken talent conversations that take place are not appropriate to record.

- Having an audio or video recording of the meeting could be intimidating to some participants, which may stifle the discussion.

- If you used this method to record the talent information, this would mean that someone would then later need to listen to the entire meeting again to glean the important information from everything stated in the meeting.

- If the recording failed in any way during the meeting, critical data would be lost.

Question: If I notify someone as a High Potential, won't I then have the difficult task of having to "de-notify" them at some point, and won't that damage their morale?

Answer: This issue is easily resolved by determining the timeframe and/or criteria for each high potential to remain as such, **and then communicating this to the High Potential population as they begin their development plan**, so they have an expectation from the beginning that they will be identified as a High Potential a for a specific period of time only.

For example, some companies notify an employee that they have been selected to participate in the High Potential program for a finite time period, such as a development program that the participant completes in a 2-year period.

In other companies, the leadership team reviews the current list of High Potentials and each and determines if they will remain in the program for another year or not. Or, the company may use specific criteria for remaining in the program and when the criteria is no longer applicable, the individual moves out of the program. It is important at that point to also offer other training development resources to this individual to ensure a continuous learning culture, and to avoid a potential morale issue.

It is also important to communicate to everyone that being identified as a High Potential is not a "stamp on the forehead for life", but a point-in-time development option. Employees will move in and move out of the High Potential population or program over time. In other words, the company is saying to the employee, "At this point in your career we see that you are demonstrating the exceptional ability and the desire for focused development and potential leadership career growth." When the High Potential employee understands this definition, it greatly reduces or eliminates any morale issues when the employee is no longer in the High Potential population.

Question: Why do I need both a Talent Assessment Process and a Talent Review Meeting?

Answer: Going into a Talent Review Meeting without any preparation (such as completing the leadership assessment process and without talking with employees about their career, relocation, and development interests) can result in a non-productive and ineffective Talent Review Meeting, where assumptions are made because factual data is not available.

Conversely, completing a leadership assessment process without the calibration process that occurs in a Talent Review Meeting results in a compiled database that has not been reviewed or validated by the leadership team. Remember, the Talent Review Meeting increases the visibility of top talent and serves to increase the validity of succession plans.

Together, the leadership assessment process and the Talent Review Meetings result in talent information that has been viewed objectively and has been approved by the entire leadership team of the functional area.

Question: How should I respond to an employee who is asking why they were not selected as a high potential?

Answer: The manager of this employee is the one who should respond to this question, providing coaching to the employee regarding the strengths they demonstrate and the development areas that may be holding the employee back from being selected as a High Potential.

This question should be handled by a manager in the same way they would handle a question such as, "Why was I not selected for the promotion I applied for?" Quite simply, the manager needs to answer the question honestly using effective coaching skills and focusing on helping the employee to leverage strengths as well as addressing development areas.

Question: What should I do in a Talent Review Meeting if the meeting moves off track?

Answer: This is a judgment call that you will need to make – if the team is discussing a critical issue that relates to the talent and succession planning strategy, and it is evident that that team needs to address this issue urgently, the best thing to do may be to not interfere at all and let the discussion progress.

However, if the discussion is something that should be taken "off line" and discussed at a later date (either because it is not relevant to the meeting or because more information needs to be gathered before a decision can be made), you can create a "parking lot" for these topics to enable the issue to be captured for later discussion, and to help the team "move on".

Question: How can I help my leaders to be more prepared for the Talent Review Meeting?

Answer: Prior to the meeting, continue to check the progress of leadership assessment completions to be sure that all are completed prior to the meeting. Communicate the meeting agenda to the Business Leaders, so they know exactly what will be discussed so they can bring the appropriate information with them, and to allow time for them to schedule discussions with employees to gather information. For example, if you expect leaders to know the relocation ability of each of their employees, make sure they are aware of this prior to the meeting so they can gather this information.

Be sure to work with the Executive Assistants of each functional area so they know the dates, locations, and other details of the meeting, so they can answer questions about the meeting if they are asked, and so they can help support the meeting by ensuring the leaders' calendars are kept clear from other scheduling conflicts.

Question: One of the managers I support has asked if she can select someone who is not in her functional area as a potential successor on her succession plan. How should I respond?

Answer: Not only is it okay for leader to identify an employee who doesn't report to him or her as a successor, it is encouraged. This practice encourages more cross-functional career movement within the organization, which builds skill sets and broadens the knowledge and perspectives of our employees.

Question: A manager is asking is he can nominate someone from another functional area as a high potential. How should I respond?

Answer: In this situation, it is best for this manager to contact the person who manages this employee directly, to communicate their idea about nominating the individual as a High Potential. It would then be up to the manager of the employee to factor in this information and determine if the employee should be nominated as a High Potential.

Question: If I am serving as the facilitator of the Talent Review Meeting and I know the employee who is being discussed in the Talent Review Meeting, should I contribute my opinions to the discussion?

Answer: It is important that you remain objective in the meeting to maintain the trust of the Business Leaders. If you break away from being objective, you run the risk of losing the trust of the leaders regarding how the data will be used – after all, if you want to modify the meeting discussion to match your own opinions, what might you do with the data after the meeting? When you begin to participate in the meeting, you break away from your role as a facilitator/partner of the meeting.

So what do you do if you are aware of a strength or development area for an employee being discussed during the meeting, and no one is mentioning it? Ask a question. Instead of supplying your opinion – "Jason has great presentation skills", you can ask, "How would you describe Jason's presentation skills, which are important for this position?" Using this method will enable you to gather data and perspectives without inserting your own opinion and losing your role as an objective facilitator.

Question: Should High Potentials and Successors be given any priority over other employees when applying for internal positions in the organization?

Answer: It is important to follow your standard internal recruiting procedure first to ensure the position is communicated to any and all qualified applicants in the organization. In conjunction with this process, it is also important to look at the succession plan and the High Potential list to ensure that candidates on this list are considered for the open position. This may include additional steps to directly communicate the vacant position to the managers of the High Potentials and Successors who were previously identified as candidates for the position, to ensure they are aware of the open position.

The recruiting team and Business Leaders should consider all candidates who are qualified for the position, whether or not they are on the high potential list or the succession plan. However, if all other factors are equal among candidates, the fact that an employee is a High Potential or is on the succession plan can certainly be used as criteria in the hiring process.

Question: An employee is asking me if he/she can apply (or self-select) for High Potential program. How should I respond?

Answer: Let the employee know that the High Potential selection process includes discussions and decisions by the leadership team and it is not a development program that employees apply to participate in. However, employees can talk with their manager about their interest in the program, to make sure their manager is aware of their interest.

Question: What if an employee is selected as a High Potential and is notified of this decision, but he/she does not want to be part of the High Potential program at this time?

Answer: Employees should not be required to be part of the High Potential program if it does not meet their current needs or situation. However, it is a good idea to talk with the employee about why they don't want to participate at this time. Frequently, the employee has a misconception about the program that is causing them to think that it won't fit into their schedule or situation at this time.

Printed in Great Britain
by Amazon.co.uk, Ltd.,
Marston Gate.